PUSSY HATS,
POLITICS, AND
PUBLIC PROTEST

PUSSY HATS, POLITICS, AND PUBLIC PROTEST

EDITED BY
RACHELLE HOPE SALTZMAN

University of Mississippi Press / Jackson

The University Press of Mississippi is the scholarly publishing agency of the Mississippi Institutions of Higher Learning: Alcorn State University, Delta State University, Jackson State University, Mississippi State University, Mississippi University for Women, Mississippi Valley State University, University of Mississippi, and University of Southern Mississippi.

www.upress.state.ms.us

The University Press of Mississippi is a member of the Association of University Presses.

First printing 2020
∞

Library of Congress Cataloging-in-Publication Data available
Hardback ISBN 978-1-4968-3156-9
Trade paperback ISBN 978-1-4968-3157-6
Epub single ISBN 978-1-4968-3158-1
Epub institutional ISBN 978-1-4968-3159-0
PDF single ISBN 978-1-4968-3160-6
PDF institutional ISBN 978-1-4968-3161-3

British Library Cataloging-in-Publication Data available

FOR OUR FOREMOTHERS AND
ALL THOSE ON WHOSE SHOULDERS WE STAND.
FOR OUR CHILDREN AND OUR GRANDCHILDREN.
FOR OUR TEACHERS, MENTORS, AND COLLEAGUES.

CONTENTS

ACKNOWLEDGMENTS

My sincerest thanks to my coauthors for their hard and dedicated work in co-creating this volume, and to all those who took part in the 2017 panels on the Women's March for the annual conference of the American Folklore Society. I wish that more of the insightful presentations could have been included. I am most grateful to all of those involved as well as friends, colleagues, and family members who took part in the marches, in person, and virtually; I speak for all the contributors in expressing appreciation for your photos, thoughts, and encouragement as we all wrote, rewrote, edited, and rewrote again our chapters for this book.

In particular, I want to acknowledge our anonymous reviewers who pushed us, sometimes painfully, to acknowledge the positionality and perspective in our chapters and in our political participation. While we didn't agree with all the reviewers' comments, they made us reach deeper and more critically to ultimately craft a better book.

My deepest thanks go to Patricia Sawin and Jack Santino for their helpful and thoughtful comments on my chapter. It's been a special privilege to collaborate with both—longtime friends and colleagues—in this effort. Our ongoing email discussions about festival theory, ritual time, and the carnivalesque have been intellectually and personally exciting and invigorating and pushed me to articulate some long-held thoughts on these topics. I also very much appreciate how they and the rest of the contributors helped to sharpen the introduction. A sincere thank you as well to Wendy Stegall, who graciously stepped in to create a far more robust index than we could have created on our own.

My appreciation goes out to the home folks, my husband, Nick Rieser, and daughter, Eva Saltzman. Besides giving up family time while I worked on this volume, both were eager participants in the 2017 Women's March and in several since. Eva, who has her own keen photographic eye, has put up with my sometimes-annoying questions about her first and subsequent marches and demonstrations. Her perspective has certainly informed mine. Nick not only provides encouragement for my work but also supplies personal tech support. He was ready with a portable charger as my phone battery died on the day of the march. And he saved the day when multiple (!) computer crashes occurred in the midst of my sending the final manuscript and photos to the publishers.

University Press of Mississippi editors Katie Keene and Mary Heath deserve much credit for the existence of *Pussy Hats, Politics, and Public Protest*. They noticed our several organized AFS panels and emailed before the conference to enquire whether we were interested in doing a book. Further thanks are due to UPM project manager, Shane Gong Stewart, and UPM's brilliant designer, Jennifer Mixon. Their cheerleading and encouragement have been invaluable as we moved through making conference presentations into what we very much hope is a book accessible to those interested in folklore and politics, women's movements, and protest and charivari.

INTRODUCTION

The 2016 presidential campaign and its aftermath provoked an array of protests remarkable for their symbolic intensity. The authors in this collection of essays focus upon the women-centered aspects of the protests that started with the 2017 Women's March. We emphasize the very public nature of that surprising, grassroots spectacle and explore the crucial relationship between the personal and the political in the protests. The very word "pussy," which so many women immediately appropriated from the 2016 Republican candidate's vulgar declarations, became central to the public debate about women's bodies and their political, social, and economic rights. The Women's March and its iterations on social media continue to resonate with associative and symbolic meaning. Women, and their multigendered compatriots, flung aside censorship and embraced, invented, and proclaimed deep and new meanings for pussies (their own and otherwise), conflating the scripts for political protest with traditional censure or charivari—a form of protest derived from ritual folk drama that frequently includes masking, parades, noisemaking, and sometimes destruction of property and/or physical violence.

Such activities have been documented as early as the seventeenth century and as recently as today (Dobash and Dobash 1981; Friedman 2018; Hobsbawm and Rudé 1975; Hunt 2017; Saltzman 1994a, 1995b; Santino 2011, 2017; Thompson 1991; Williams 1971).

The historical purpose of charivari or rough musicking (Alford 1959; Beik 2007; Johnson 1990) was to sanction and censure, to protest incursions against a popularly agreed-upon notion of social justice. People tend to invoke more symbolically loaded critique when legal recourse has not addressed perceived wrongs. In centuries past, the so-called crowd tarred and feathered impolitic politicians or those who violated social norms in some way (Hobsbawm and Rudé 1975; Saltzman 1994a) or drowned out political speakers with the age-old method of rough musicking—loud noises, boos, or catcalls—to critique, censure, and even censor. On occasion—both then and more recently—they flouted unpopular laws—by striking and demonstrating; donning "Indian" disguise and dumping tea into Boston Harbor in 1773; occupying a federal wildlife refuge and federal offices (Malheur Wildlife Refuge in Oregon) in 2016 (Walker 2018); donning *gilet jaune*, the fluorescent yellow hazard vest, and marching in the streets of France to protest unfair fuel prices in 2018 (Friedman 2018); or banging pots and pans in a march to demand the resignation of Wanda Vásquez from her position as Puerto Rico's secretary of justice as well as her withdrawal from her pending post as governor of the territory (Robles 2019).

In the past, women's activities during popular protests have been approved when they have supported a male majority or when the issues at stake have to do with the domestic sphere and/or stereotypical caretaking and nurturing roles—food (Blood and Bread Riots of 1789), children (Child Labor Laws), education, temperance, and such (NOW 2019). When women "overstep"—as in demonstrations and protests for voting and property rights, for sovereignty over their own bodies, or against other pillars of the status quo—we are deemed unruly, unfit, even unnatural (Vogelstein and Turkington 2017). And when men disguise themselves as women to protest, they do so in the shadows or at night (David 1971) in order to mask their identities and sometimes to dodge responsibility for their actions, but most of all to point to the "unnatural" behavior when those in power seem to violate a perceived notion of a social contract. When men dress as women "in fun," they tend to do so as a critique of women's violation of their social/domestic duties, as in mummers plays, womanless weddings (McCracken 2001), or drag (Cracker 2015). Parody and humor can thus be dismissed as "only joking" (Marsh 2015; Smith and Saltzman 1995). While the Women's March participants may have co-opted the techniques of parody and punning to make their points, they meant their multivocalic messages in all seriousness and specifically challenged the idea that it might be unnatural or improper for women to stand up for their rights.

That said, what marked the 2017 Women's March as a qualitatively different kind of protest were the sheer numbers of women and their allies who joined together as a seemingly united intersectional whole to say "hell, no" to incursions on their bodies, their rights, and those of other women, children, Native American sovereignty, Black and Brown bodies, and a host of others who had been violated by the 2016 presidential election and what its results seemed to portend. And they did it not in disguise or in the shadows, but in the full light of day, along the public streets, in small towns and major cities around the world to declare a president unfit and his government's agenda illegitimate.

Particularly striking about the Women's March and its expansion to every state in the Union as well as in countries worldwide were the numbers—with estimates ranging from 4.5 million (Pressman and Chenoweth 2017) up to 5 million worldwide (Women's March Organizers 2018: 216). When there is a public march, size matters, as Santino notes in his chapter; large scale is an indicator of representation or acceptance. Most predictions low-balled participation; even organizers expected only a quarter of those who actually turned out. The unprecedented and parallel rise of the private Facebook group Pantsuit Nation, which has had as many as 3.3 million members and, at this writing (April 27, 2020), 3.1 million members, amplified the sense of a national group of likeminded people. Such numbers speak loudly and in contrast to the low turnout for the 2017 inauguration day event on the National Mall. According to the authors of *Together We Rise*, there were more than three times as many people marching in Washington, DC, on January 21, 2017, than had been present for the presidential inauguration the day before (2018).

These public displays also cut across generations and ethnicities. Participants actively invoked the spirit of inclusion—for (almost) all and for all issues that spoke to the expansive and welcoming zeitgeist of the day and the weeks that followed. There was some dissent during the planning stages over leadership and membership, as well as the exclusion of certain topics: anti-abortion speakers were not invited as official participants for the Washington, DC, march; there were not originally accommodations for the other-abled; and there was conflict at that same march over whether Jewish women could carry flags bearing the Star of David. Such divisions lost pertinence during the actual marches. Since 2017, however, more has been made of those divisions, resulting in dual marches in some cities in subsequent years and the withdrawal of individual states and cities from the national organization (McSweeney and Siegel 2018; Stockman 2018). While the American women's movement as a whole has been critiqued for not being particularly diverse in terms of ethnicity and income level, those charges were not at issue among the general public—at least not in January 2017.

During those January 2017 marches, public displays were in evidence, with the material aspect of the Women's March front and center. Women have historically used color, pins, and ribbons to express support for causes, such as the gold (and later white and purple) of the American suffragettes, lavender for GLBTQ+ protests, or pink for supporters of Planned Parenthood (Blakemore 2019; Friedman 2018; Pershing and Yocom 1996; Wikipedia n.d.). The women involved have created and maintained opportunities for storytelling, advocacy, and community building. Making, sharing, and displaying material culture, particularly handmade hats and signs, related to the 2017 Women's March created community, engaged participants with craft, and created visual and material icons of resistance (Women's March Organizers 2018:83–90, 257).

It is a bit of a truism to note that interest groups have always marched in support of causes, but most protest marches have not been imbued with the intensity of carnivalesque behavior (Santino 2017) that characterized the 2017 Women's March. In identifying this specific type of protest, we invoke the spirit of both revelry and social critique that festivals like Mardi Gras, Carnival, Purim, or Halloween embody. There is a festival license to do and say risqué things, to articulate even dangerous and threatening ideas, during those times that sanction public play, parody, and social critique. The moments of exhilarated oneness, of *communitas* (Turner 1974:76–77) among those carried along by the energy of the crowd, also transmit great potential for social change that can spill over into the everyday. Part of the energy of the carnivalesque comes from its ability to bring together seemingly unrelated issues and movements from across the sociopolitical spectrum. It is this union of disparate parts that creates the potential for real social transformation. In sum, the deep feeling of oneness and belief in change can lead us to actuate change, as evidenced by the 2018 mid-term elections that returned not only a majority of Democrats to the US House but an unprecedented number of women and women of color.

To be sure, the Parkland shooting in a Florida high school and the subsequent protests against gun violence that the young and brave survivors of that shooting have led have not yet resulted in the hoped-for changes to US gun laws; yet numerous instances since of white supremacist terrorism, resulting most recently in massacres in El Paso, Texas, and Dayton, Ohio, have spurred considerable momentum for banning assault weapons and conducting mandatory background checks.[1] The #MeToo movement has had more singular successes as years of sexual abuse in Hollywood, industry, politics, and even the Catholic Church have brought down those once viewed as impervious. The Confederate monuments on the south mall at the University of Texas at Austin are no more (Rhodes 2019). Silent Sam finally came down on the UNC Chapel Hill campus as often violent demonstrations between white supremacists of different types and minorities (and their allies) protested racist tropes and behavior. During 2019 there was a movement afoot to remove the pioneer statues (toppled June 2020) at the University of Oregon, which recently renamed a building that once commemorated a Ku Klux Klan leader. For the very first time in the US, significant numbers of women won elected offices in local, state, and national midterm races. Over one hundred women of diverse cultural backgrounds now sit in the US Congress. Stacy Abrams, an African American woman, nearly became the governor of Georgia (there is still debate about the actual outcome of that election and evidence of voter fraud piles up). *That* is real change that we are now seeing, along with several new agendas to ameliorate climate change and more. Of course, those on the other side are also fighting for change; new legislation in eleven states so far that would criminalize abortion, the president's efforts to deport DACA residents, the inhumane separation of children and families at the US-Mexico border, and ICE raids in towns and cities throughout the country make it clear that deep-seated divisions continue to divide American society.

As folklorists we've been schooled to recognize cultural patterns and instances of traditional expressive culture. It's just icing on the cake when we spot them as part of a symbolic protest, especially one in which we've taken part. Parades have long provided space and time for affirming civic hierarchy and order as well as to celebrate an ideal vision of society (Darnton 1984; Davis 1986; Glassberg 1990). Protest marches take parades as their model and upend the orderly proceedings that characterize parades. Instead of playing out a narrative about social hierarchy and place with appropriate groups of participants that process in a seemingly logical order in front of cheering crowds, protest marches involve not a linear procession but surging groups, chants, sometimes songs, signage, and a disorderly conclusion. Creative and colorful protest signs and the ubiquitous pussy hat particularly distinguished the 2017 women's marches and other protests against the 2016 presidential election.

The material spaces of the marches—whether in stores, at the marches themselves, on social media or other online spaces, and elsewhere—as well as the material objects themselves, reflected and were challenged by racial, personal, and generational differences. This focus brings to light questions concerning whose stories get to be told, sanctioned, and studied and whose do not, along with creating a space to discuss how women's folk culture, particularly material artifacts and art, can serve as a means for resistance and protest, building alliances and expanding narratives to be inclusive of all. For many of those who wore them, the pussy hats, pins, charms, and the like provided the wearers and those observing them an opportunity to seek common ground, though women of color and others who identify as female have also critiqued the use of the color pink in reference to female genitalia and even the concept of "pussy" (Women's March Organizers 2018:257). The social action projects described in the chapters in this volume demonstrate the importance of identity politics and place-based identity, and question the points of intersection between lesbian and feminist communities in Lancaster, feminist and women of color communities in Chicago, and the community of crafters and a variety of participants worldwide.

The chapters that follow explore different aspects of the 2017 Women's March and seek to elucidate the persistence of the carnivalesque, multivocality, and *communitas*—and their power to effect real change through their ability to point out the rents in our social fabric.

Jack Santino's "Pussies Galore! Women, Power, and Protest at the 2017 March" looks at the Washington, DC, march to analyze how all dimensions in a public manifestation take on symbolic meaning. In the case of the historic 2017 Women's March on Washington, the timing (the day after the inauguration) and place (the National Mall) both communicated direct opposition to the legitimization of Donald Trump. Along with the central, newly emergent symbol of the pussy hat, the very nature of the protest as a women's march (despite the welcome participation of men) constructed women themselves, and their bodies, their sexuality, and their agency as primary symbolic forces aimed at countering the regressive hypermasculinity embodied in the candidate and now president.

My own chapter, "These Pussies Grab Back: Protesting at the 2017 Portland Women's March," focuses on the march in Portland, Oregon, where over 100,000 women and their allies of all ages and genders showed up for a festive, public display event. My analysis looks in particular at how the march included the traditional features of public display events: chants, rhyming slogans, costumes, and noisemaking. I look especially at the handmade signs and the ways in which their vernacular art typified the multivocality of the carnivalesque. I also explore the transformational role such moments play in creating structural change.

In "Pussy Hats: Common Ground at the Chicago Women's March," Susan Eleuterio focuses on the pussy hats that became a symbol of resistance. They displayed unified opposition to the stated goals of the Trump administration and, at the same time, uniquely individual expressions. She notes that the stylized hats served as a way for women to feel "connected, protected, and activated," virtually, physically, and over time and space in the greater Chicago region. Those who chose to wear pussy hats used a range of colors and styles. Part of the community building before, during, and after the march centered on the giving and sharing of hats (and other material culture, such as pins), which is something characteristic of many women's friendships. Men also give gifts, but the idea of a handmade gift has been part of women's culture for many decades in America. Women's stories about their not-always-pink hats document community building and ongoing activism, and reflect the unique experience of each woman.

Taking a closer look at the varieties of material culture that the women's march generated, Andrea Glass writes of "Postcards, Pussy Hats, and Protest Pins: Documenting the Folklore of Feminist Resistance at Mio Studio in Lancaster." Mio Studio was an LGBT-owned and woman-owned art gallery in downtown Lancaster that became the center for the gallery artists' social action projects. Amplifying Eleuterio's take on the way hats generated stories and thus affirmed community for the women involved, Glass argues that that those artistic social action projects sparked opportunities for women to gather and exchange stories. A new material culture of resistance simultaneously developed that was both part of larger national trends and uniquely local. The oral transmission of stories allowed participants to heal, feel empowered, and receive direction for future action. She concludes that grassroots movements provide a framework for documenting a larger folklore of resistance.

Adam Zolkover's essay "Paid and Professional Protesters? Giving Voice to Trump Resisters" provides another take on grassroots efforts. Zolkover has examined some of the ways in which Republican leaders and right-leaning media floated stories claiming that protestors had been paid, sometimes funded by George Soros, sometimes working for Barack Obama. The "logic" behind such claims was that gatherings like the Women's March have been suspiciously large and that activists are, by definition, fringe, but those involved in the Women's March and subsequent protests are not. Zolkover maintains that while this perspective posits a false and dehumanizing narrative, it also embeds a host of traditional elements that animate its rhetorical power for Trump supporters. Ironically, this "fake news" actually animated some protestors who would otherwise never have been involved. Zolkover includes interviews with two women who were not politically active before the 2016 election but who, when faced with a crisis in competence in the new regime and with the claim that protestors were motivated by payment rather than conviction, have found their public political voice.

Our collection concludes with Patricia Sawin's "'I Can't Believe I Still Have to Protest This Shit': Generational Variation and Solidarity among Women's March Participants," a title that pretty much sums up our collective response to the 2016 election and the administration's undemocratic actions since. Sawin argues that the 2017 Women's March was an emphatic show of intergenerational solidarity, evidence that women and allies across the age spectrum objected to the sexism, racism, ageism, ableism, and xenophobia; the lack of intelligence, good judgment, and simple humanity; and the appalling policy proposals of the man who had just been inaugurated president. As Sawin notes, marchers of different ages did not all play the same role. She identifies four approximate generational cohorts and argues that the recognizable role each played was a distinctive symbolic component of the march's overall message and effect. Each cohort had a distinctive part to play in claiming space, refuting slurs, and asserting the right of women to be themselves and to be valued and respected at every age.

In hindsight we've all realized that the enthusiastic groundswell of protest marked the beginning of what has become a multivocal, multiclass, multiracial, and multigendered movement to call out the hypocrisies in our democratic republic. The 2017 global women's marches protesting the ascendancy of the Trump administration seem to have amplified grassroots support for change—from #MeToo to #Parkland, from #ThisisMyLane to #TakeaKnee and countless others—protests against so many outrages have seemed nonstop since November 2016, and they have indeed tested our capacity. This current year, 2019, has brought to a head the travesty of asylum seekers' illegal imprisonment on the US southern border, ICE raids, ongoing legislative challenges to *Roe v. Wade*, and more—each with its attendant public demonstrations, marches, and social media outrage. The summer brought Trump's co-optation of the annual July Fourth Independence Day celebration on the National Mall and his subsequent speech gaffes that revealed quite stunning ignorance about American history (Walsh 2019). And in September, when the Category 5 Hurricane Dorian struck the Bahamas, the president apparently illegally altered a NOAA weather map with a Sharpie marker to inexplicably and repeatedly insist that Alabama lay in the storm's path (Milbank 2019). Each outrage brought a new wave of comedic memes, whose biting satire provided a brief antidote to the atrocities and overtook Facebook, Twitter, and Instagram to signify how out of place so many find Trump and his vision of this country.

Despite how distractingly appealing the outrages and creative responses have been, it's important to remember that in the days leading up to the 2016 US presidential election and the marches that followed, no one could foresee that the 2017 women's marches were just the beginning and not a culmination of a collective frustration with the American political system. The January 2017 women's marches provided a moment of exhilaration, a time when many of us who'd never marched before and those who had never stopped came out almost unbidden to join together. In particular and in contrast to publications such as *Together We Rise: Behind the Scenes at the Protest Heard around the World* (2018), our essays speak to the experiences of regular, rather than leading, participants. We do not purport to cover all perspectives in terms of gender identity, ethnicity, and social class; what we do offer is the perspective of a folkloric lens and some of the ways in which it can enable us to recognize the pervasive symbolic systems that, in certain moments, realign and provide models and inspiration for systemic change.

Note

1. At this writing in April 2020, the US House of Representatives has passed a bill calling for both measures, but the US Senate under the leadership of Senator Mitch McConnell has yet to allow a vote to come to the floor of the Senate on S. 66, Assault Weapons Ban of 2019.

Works Cited

Alford, Violet. 1959. Rough Music or Charivari. *Folklore* 70(4):505–18.

Beik, William 2007. The Violence of the French Crowd from Charivari to Revolution. *Past and Present* 197(1):75–110.

Blakemore, Erin. 2019. The Many Meanings of Yellow Ribbons. *JSTOR Daily*. April 26. https://daily.jstor.org/the-many-meanings-of-yellow-ribbons/.

Cracker, Miz. 2015. Drag Isn't Like Blackface. But That Doesn't Mean It's Always Kind to Women. *Slate*. February 17. https://slate.com/human-interest /2015/02/is-mary-cheney-right-about-drag-being-like-blackface.html.

Darnton, Robert. 1984. *The Great Cat Massacre*. New York: Basic Books.

Davis, Susan. 1986. *Parades and Power*. Philadelphia: University of Pennsylvania Press.

Dobash, Russell P., and R. Emerson Dobash. 1981. Community Response to Violence against Wives: Charivari, Abstract Justice and Patriarchy. *Social Problems* 28(5):563–81.

Glassberg, David. 1990. *American Historical Pageantry*. Chapel Hill: University of North Carolina Press.

Hunt, Tamara. 2017. "The Prince of Whales": Caricature, Charivari, and the Politics of Morality. In *Splendidly Victorian*, edited by Michael H. Shirley and Todd E. A. Larson, 21–54. London: Routledge.

Friedman, Vanessa. 2018. The Power of the Yellow Vests. *New York Times*. December 4. https://www.nytimes.com/2018/12/04/fashion/yellow-vests -france-protest-fashion.html?emc=edit_nn_p_20181227&module=inline &nl=morning-briefing&nlid=70764435mp&section=backStory&te=1.

Hobsbawm, Eric, and George Rudé. 1975. *Captain Swing*. London: W. W. Norton.

Johnson, Loretta T. 1990. Charivari/Shivaree: A European Folk Ritual on the American Plains. *Journal of Interdisciplinary History* 20(3):371–87.

Marsh, Moira. 2015. *Practically Joking*. Logan: Utah State University Press

McCracken, Elizabeth. 2001. The Womanless Wedding. *Columbia: A Journal of Literature and Art* 35:25–38. http://www.jstor.org/stable/41808064.s

McSweeney, Leah, and Jacob Siegel. 2018. Is the Women's March Melting Down? *Tablet*. December 10. https://www.tabletmag.com/jewish-news-and-politics /276694/is-the-womens-march-melting-down.

Milbank, Dana. 2019. Donald and the Black Sharpie. *Washington Post*. September 9. https://www.washingtonpost.com/opinions/donald-and-the-black-sharpie /2019/09/06/44202240-d0b9–11e9-b29b-a528dc82154a_story.html.

NOW. n.d. History of Marches and Mass Actions. NOW. https://now.org/about /history/history-of-marches-and-mass-actions (access date April 21, 2020).

Pershing, Linda, and Margaret R. Yocom. 1996. The Yellow Ribboning of the USA: Contested Meanings in the Construction of a Political Symbol. *Western Folklore* 55(1):41–85. doi:10.2307/1500148.

Pressman, Jeremy, and Erica Chenoweth. 2017. Women's March Attendance Estimate Spreadsheet (closed January 26, 2017; accessed October 14, 2017). https://docs.google.com/spreadsheets/d/1xaoiLqYKz8x9Yc_rfhtmSOJQ2E GgeUVjvV4A8LsIaxY/htmlview?sle=true#gid=0.

Rhodes, Diane. 2019. Empty Pedestals: Belonging on the South Mall. Medium. June 24. https://medium.com/@dm.diane/empty-pedestals-belonging-on -the-south-mall-643cda95d529.

Robles, Frances. 2019. Protests Are Still Erupting in Puerto Rico: This Time, It's over Wanda Vazquez as Governor. *New York Times*. July 29. https://www .nytimes.com/2019/07/29/us/puerto-rico-march-vazquez-rossello.html.

Saltzman, Rachelle H. 1994a. Calico Indians and Pistol Pills: Historical Symbols and Political Action. *New York Folklore* 20(3–4):1–18.

Saltzman, Rachelle H. 1994b. Folklore as Politics in Great Britain: Working-Class Critiques of Upper-Class Strike Breakers in the 1926 General Strike. *Anthropological Quarterly: Symbols of Contention, Part II* (Special Issue) 67(3):105–21.

Saltzman, Rachelle H. 1995a. Public Displays, Play, and Power: The 1926 General Strike. *Southern Folklore: Façade Performances* (Special Issue) 52(2):161–86.

Saltzman, Rachelle H. 1995b. "This Buzz Is for You": Popular Responses to the Ted Bundy Execution. *Journal of Folklore Research: "Arbiters of Taste: Censuring/Censoring Discourse"* (Special Issue) 32(2):101–20.

Saltzman, Rachelle H. 2012. *A Lark for the Sake of Their Country: The 1926 General Strike Volunteers in Folklore and Memory.* Manchester: Manchester University Press.

Santino, Jack. 2011. The Carnivalesque and the Ritualesque. *Journal of American Folklore* 124(491):61–73. doi:10.5406/jamerfolk.124.491.0061.

Santino, Jack. 2017. *Public Performances: Studies in the Carnivalesque and Ritualesque.* Logan: Utah State University Press.

Smith, Moira, and Rachelle H Saltzman. 1995. Introduction to Tastelessness. "Arbiters of Taste: Censuring/Censoring Discourse." Special issue, *Journal of Folklore Research:* 32(2):85–100.

S. 66—116th Congress: Assault Weapons Ban of 2019. www.GovTrack.us. 2019. April 21, 2020. https://www.govtrack.us/congress/bills/116/s66.

Stockman, Farah. 2018. Women's March Roiled by Accusations of Anti-Semitism. *New York Times.* December 23. https://www.nytimes.com/2018/12/23/us /womens-march-anti-semitism.html.

Thompson, Edward P. 1991. *Customs in Common.* New York: New Press.

Vogelstein, Rachel, and Rebecca Turkington. 2017. Five Women's Marches throughout History That Triggered Political Change. The Lily. https://www

.thelily.com/five-womens-marches-throughout-history-that-triggered-poli
tical-change/.

Walker, Peter. 2018. *Sagebrush Collaboration: How Harney County Defeated the Takeover of the Malheur Wildlife Refuge*. Corvallis: Oregon State University Press.

Walsh, Lara. 2019. The Tweets about Trump's Fourth of July Speech & Parade Call Out This Blunder. *Elite Daily*. July 5. https://www.elitedaily.com/p/the-tweets-about-trumps-fourth-of-july-speech-parade-call-out-this-blunder-18172533.

Wikipedia. List of Awareness Ribbons. https://en.wikipedia.org/wiki/List_of_awareness_ribbons. last edited March 28, 2020, at 15:33 (UTC).

Williams, David. 1971. *The Rebecca Riots A Study in Agrarian Dissent*. Cardiff: University of Wales Press.

Women's March Organizers and Condé Nast. 2018. *Together We Rise: The Women's March: Behind the Scenes at the Protest Heard around the World*. New York: Dey Street Books.

PUSSY HATS,
POLITICS, AND
PUBLIC PROTEST

PUSSIES GALORE

WOMEN, POWER, AND PROTEST
IN THE AGE OF TRUMP

Jack Santino

The Women's March of January 2017 was, by many accounts, one of the largest, if not the largest, mass demonstration in US history. Although clearly influenced directly by previous political actions such as the 1963 March on Washington, the Million Man March, and the Million Mom March, the Women's March took place in its own specific historical moment—one represented by the election of Donald Trump to the US presidency. The Women's March has served as a new paradigm for female empowerment and has spawned follow-up marches, including a national gun control demonstration following a mass shooting at a Florida high school in 2018. My chapter analyzes the Women's March in the context of previous research on public assembly and performative actions of grievance and censure—and in the particular context of the Trump presidential campaign and inauguration.

To say that Trump is a polarizing figure is an understatement. During his presidential campaign against other Republican candidates, and then against former secretary of state Hillary Clinton, Trump was seen ridiculing a reporter with a physical handicap; he directly insulted all Americans of Mexican descent; he was endorsed by the Ku Klux Klan; and he made innuendoes that a reporter was having her period during a presidential debate. During debates with Clinton, he moved into her area of the stage and hovered, glowering, behind her. He is overwhelming in his social transgressions, and a great many of these indicate hostility toward women in any role other than sexual object. It is perhaps, then, no surprise that his victory in the Electoral College (he lost the popular vote by a substantial margin to Clinton) sparked a widespread movement loosely called "the Resistance."

Perhaps the Occupy movement and, especially, Black Lives Matter can be viewed as immediate precursors to the wider Resistance; although the Arab Spring must be seen as the first mass resistance of the twenty-first century. Historian Lucy Barber (2004) traces marches on Washington to 1884; the 1963 March on Washington and the 1968 Poor People's March, along with the moratoriums directed against the Vietnam War, are perhaps the most widely recognized protest marches in American history. As in all such rituals of protest preceding, people called attention to their grievances by their physical presence. For instance, influenced perhaps by the Arab Spring demonstrations, in the Occupy movement people came and stayed, camping out, eating, and sleeping at significant sites. Occupy was largely a protest against neoliberalism and its political allies; people literally occupied a site day and night as a means of calling attention to their grievances. Black Lives Matter is an ongoing struggle that took its shape after so many police shootings of unarmed Black men went unaccounted for. In this latter case, African Americans took to the streets and announced that they simply would not allow it to go on. To say, "Black lives matter," is a way of saying we are people, too. Demonstrating en masse is another way of asserting personhood and personal value through spectacular presence.

When Trump was elected, it was a woman's movement, fittingly, that responded to his extremism. The march of 2017 was by no means the first such action by women; it was not even the first Women's March. The Women's March to Versailles, in October 1789, resulted when the women of the Paris markets, tired of high prices, set out on foot to the palace of Versailles. There, having been joined by the Marquis de Lafayette, they persuaded King Louis XVI and Queen Marie Antoinette to return with them to Paris as prisoners. Despite some failed escape attempts, the two never returned to Versailles and were eventually beheaded. While these events cannot be said to be a direct precursor to the recent Women's March on Washington, they were certainly precedents (see Beik 2007; Jarvis 2019). In more recent years, there have been several female-led public protest marches, such as the Million Mom March, Slut Walks, and lesbian demonstrations (see Currans 2017), as well as the Madres de la Plaza demonstrations in Chile and Argentina, and even the Pussy Riot actions in Russia. It is my belief that, along with these others, the Women's March was a cultural milestone. I believe such women-centric and performative public actions will continue to be of particular significance.

The Women's March 2017

In public protest gatherings, people find it necessary to speak not only with their voices but with words and gestures, embodied and material. They speak also with their very presence. At the Women's March, the multitude of women's and men's bodies gathered spectacularly for all to witness was a performance of rejection, of censure, of opposition, but also a demonstration of an alternative, an enactment of ways of being together with other human beings. There are those who have said the Women's March was focused entirely on a negative anti-Trump message, but I would argue that the massive gathering was a display of a worldview that values diversity, creativity, inclusivity, equality—a very positive worldview that was realized in the manifestation of hundreds of thousands of people demonstrating together as individuals in consort with others. It is the mass coming-together of bodies of all types, people of many backgrounds and identities, that makes that statement: the bodies are the medium; the demonstration or manifestation is its own genre. Like festival, the protest demonstration is a genre made up of other genres (song, music, procession, flags, etc.) and involves many dimensions, all of them symbolic and significant. For example, one can consider size, composition, timing, material environment, and symbols employed.

Size

In a demonstration of this type, size matters. Such movements that stake a claim to popular representation (I regret the acceptance of the term "populist" to refer exclusively to the extreme right-wing political movements we are seeing in the US and abroad). The more sizable the turnout, the stronger the claim. The number of participants acts as an index to "the people." In mass demonstrations the participants display themselves—they intend themselves to be seen, as a way of legitimizing the underlying claim that they are representative of a larger abstraction called "the people." It is important that there be many participants, and that this large number of participants be seen.

In this regard the Women's March was a stunning success. Estimates of crowds in Washington, DC, range from 450,000 to 500,000. Millions of people demonstrated throughout the United States and internationally as well. The importance of this aspect of the event is illustrated by Trump's insistence that he had the largest crowds ever assembled for his inauguration the day before (demonstrably false), and that his crowds were larger than the Women's March (also false). It seems that size matters a great deal to Donald Trump (bodily imagery will be addressed below).

Composition

Inclusivity in the Women's March was just as important as the sheer number of participants. In the years since the first Women's March in 2017, much has been noted regarding the racial composition of the participants. While intersectionality—the recognition of mutual problems and experiences, and goals and purpose—is recognized as important, there has been less enthusiasm among African American women for the march itself (see Cho, Crenshaw, and McCall 2013). Moreover, charges of racism and anti-Semitism have arisen. An issue arose with Black Lives Matter—participants and organizers felt that being invited to the party after all their manifestations were ignored by white folks was insulting. They have a point. Issues of inclusivity, and of focusing on issues relevant to people of many different backgrounds, have long plagued women's movements. For instance, according to Elizabeth Currans, the March for Women's Lives in 2004 initially segregated Black and Latina women according to the messages on their signs; that march was critiqued as being concerned with white, middle-class women's issues exclusively (Currans 2017:120). If a demonstration is to signify inclusion of many different people's backgrounds, including race, as well as gender identity, body type, age, ethnicity, and so forth, people of those types need to feel represented and welcome to be present. Bridges have to be built, efforts made to create real diversity, real inclusivity. The Trump regime has shown hostility to many different categories of people. He has actively done away with legislation aimed at equality for the LGBTQ community, African Americans, Latinos, poor people who need health care, people with disabilities, and on and on.

Each of these groups may have its own particular issues, and there may be disagreements and misunderstandings among constituent memberships. But if one metamessage of a mass gathering during a time of purposeful political division is the presentation of an alternative model of being, one in which mutual respect and acceptance are dominant values, then the inclusion of diverse and multiple groups is crucial. In this medium of public performance, presence is necessary. It is not enough to agree with the principles and goals presented—this is the flaw in the case of Black Lives Matter. White people "supported" the protests without ever thinking of joining them. There are, in fact, many groups that have felt left out not only of neoliberalist policy but also of so-called progressive thought. All who share in being the recipients of Trump's glare, his hostility, are, to refer to Judith Butler, precarious (2015). A mass demonstration such as the Women's March seeks to assemble multiple groups whose shared quality is that of precarity.

Timing

The timing of the march is also an important dimension. Coming as it did the day after the inauguration, the Women's March presented itself as a kind of alternative inauguration, as well as a reminder to Trump, to the participants themselves, and to observers that the values that Trump represented had not succeeded in displacing and would not smother the values of inclusivity and diversity. As Judith Butler says, "Political claims are made by bodies as they appear and act, as they refuse, and as they persist, under conditions in which that fact alone threatens the state with delegitimation" (2015:83). Among other things, the Women's March said to Trump: there are more of us than there are of you.

Material Environment

Finally, the place where the event occurs is symbolically important. It took place in precisely the same place the inauguration did, the National Mall, on politically sacred ground amidst sacred national symbols of the American democratic ideal. This symbolism is always compelling, but in this particular context, the Women's March might be read as a reclaiming of these symbols, and the ideals for which they stand, back from the narrow, xenophobic, militaristic, and white supremacist readings the Trump administration campaigned on, delineated in his inauguration speech, and was about to put in place.

A word on performativity: I use the word to mean more than simply performance, taking my cue from J. L. Austin. He described "performative utterances" as speech acts that make things happen socially, for example, "I now pronounce you a wedded couple" (Austin 1962). Likewise, the Women's March was not merely a festive gathering, despite the carnivalesque bodily imagery it manifested. It was, in that sense, carnivalesque, but its purpose was to actively impact everyday life and culture. Like ritual, it was transformative and transformational in nature: the world does not simply return to the "right-side-up" after the carnivalesque inversions. Rather, the intent is to have a direct and lasting effect on the social life that continues after the event concludes. This I call ritualesque (Santino 2017), and the Women's March was a brilliant example of such.

Symbols—Pussy Hats

I've been speaking about values, clashes of values, and ways of "speaking" with voice and body, and with material objects such as signs. At the Women's March, most famously, apparel became the most visible and central symbol: hats. Pussy hats.

The pussy hats were not without controversy. Before the march, many women objected to them for many reasons—women shouldn't be associated only with their genitalia; the pink hats were too "girlish"; or the term "pussy" was offensive, not suitable for children; it was even said that the hats resembled a woman's reproductive system (anonymous personal communication Feb. 2019). In reality, of course, the use of the term "pussy" is a classic example of a subaltern group seizing a taboo word used as a weapon of superiority and control by those in a dominant position and reversing its value, thus seizing control and power. Like "Black" or "queer," the word was suddenly used against those who, like Trump, saw women only as pussies to be grabbed at (his) will. Moreover, the mass use of the reappropriated word served as a constant reminder that it was Trump, not the marchers, who had first introduced the word into this particular discourse. He had been caught bragging on tape that he was so rich, so famous, so powerful, that he could molest women with impunity. Later he dismissed this as "locker room talk." A crucial point, however, was that he had been talking not of attraction but of his own personal power to impose himself on others without their consent. He was bragging about himself and how he could do whatever he wanted to anyone he wanted. This was a strongly antiwoman statement, and it did not go unnoticed.

When we speak of carnivalesque bodily imagery, as suggested in the groundbreaking work of Mikhail Bakhtin (1968), we are speaking almost exclusively of the male realm. Bakhtin notes that carnival foolery often involves reference to the "lower bodily stratum." Here he is referring to costuming that includes oversized phalluses, or men with swollen, pregnant wombs. Both the breaking of social taboos (including reference to defecation) and inversive categorical violations (e.g., male-female) are at work here. In all of these, traditionally and historically, female genitalia have not been seen in carnival imagery.

It is very possible that we are witnessing a new development in carnivalesque display. Alina Mansfield (2017) has pointed out that at the Women's March, along with the reclaiming of the term "pussy," female genitalia were frequently depicted on signs and placards, often realistically depicted. This development may have its roots in earlier phenomena such as the successful public stagings of Eve Ensler's play *The Vagina Monologues* (1996), and the subsequent development of "V-Day" in February as a day devoted to exposing the problems of domestic violence. Both of these creations unapologetically put the word "vagina" into public discourse, and both insist on honest and frank exploration of women, sexuality, pleasure, and violence. Likewise, those interventions were met with some of the same criticisms that greeted the pussy hats—that it was counterproductive to equate or reduce women to their reproductive organs. Thus, again there is a precedent, or a context, in which emerges a symbolic discourse. It is at the 2017 Women's March that we see, perhaps for the first time, a mass display of female genitalia used as carnivalesque masquerade and costuming (see photos <40b, 41, 45, and 66> on pages 000, 000, 000, and 000 in Saltzman's and 000, 000, and 000<7, 8, and 10> in Sawin's chapters). This reflects the female authorship of the imagery and further reinforces the event as a female counterstatement to the Trump victory.

The hats, homemade and handcrafted, emerged as the primary symbol of the Women's March: embodied material culture representing women, representing true sexuality, of course, and also fecundity, fertility, reproduction, life—the real physical power of women that the Trump objectification denies and might very well be afraid of. And, of course, he ran against Hillary Clinton, who would have been the first female American president and who was the first woman presidential candidate for a major American political party. Thus, the ultimate dimension of the Women's March became the women themselves, who asserted their presence and power to lead the Resistance.

Currans points out that public space traditionally is seen as a male domain, while women are relegated to the domestic. The rise of women-centered protest events represents a real inversion, women asserting power in and by claiming public space as theirs to recontextualize by speaking out on public issues of importance to them (Currans 2017:132). In the face of Trump's insistence on reaffirming what many consider a toxic masculinity, it was an almost cosmic rebalancing, an equal and opposite reaction, that the resistance be led by and in the image of women. Trump talks about women as trophies ("she was married, but I was on her like a bitch"), his own daughter as a sexual object defined by her body ("a piece of ass"). He even referred to the size of his penis during a presidential debate. This physical imagery has always been present in his speech. Additionally, he likes to present himself as a man of violence ("I'd like to punch him in the mouth, I really would"). He has complained that attempts to lower the rate of concussions in the NFL were ruining the game; he presents himself as a tough guy. Against this, we saw an uprising of women, who, in their pluralistic public performance, posited inclusivity, multiplicity, diversity, cooperation—all as a female counterstatement to the public performances of Donald J. Trump.

The Carnivalesque and the Ritualesque

Scholars sometimes talk about the need for post-Bakhtinian approaches to carnival. I have often felt that many carnival analyses stop at the identification of Bakhtinian categories of the carnivalesque. I suggest that often the carnivalesque is put to work to accomplish long-term social goals, unlike the more usual "time out of time" model we usually employ. And when that is the case, I suggest, we are in the realm of the ritualesque. Because they are quite often festive and employ carnivalesque tropes, ritualesque events are often misunderstood—their seriousness of purpose is obscured by the obvious carnivalesque activities. The challenge is to recognize this additional dimension found in some public events, such as Pride Day, and to determine to what extent events such as carnival (with its political satire and parody) or Halloween in the US, or other events, contain ritualesque dimensions, or are ritualesque at their core.

Again, however, it is important to note that a carnivalesque event is not necessarily a *carnival*. Rough music—the ritualized public censuring of people who defy a community's sense of decency—or charivari, which is also associated with the wedding rite of passage, are carnivalesque, but they are not carnival (Alford 1959; Davis 1975; Greenhill 2010; Thompson 1971). With the Women's March of 2017, we see a mass demonstration of censure, a kind of charivari writ large; and we witness the use of carnivalesque modalities to express this disapproval. Yet the march was not a carnival in the strict sense of the term; like charivari and unlike purely festive carnival, the Women's March was intended as a necessary public construction of an alternative to the newly elected power structure. There are significant overlaps between the two phenomena, carnival and political demonstrations, and significant distinctions as well. To the extent that we can delineate them, we will be able to more accurately analyze and comprehend large public performances according to their own designs and purposes.

The 2017 Women's March was a charivari on a mass scale, and on women's terms. Using time-honored processes of carnivalesque inversion and protest, women reclaimed national symbols—the very symbols that validate the US democracy—and we witnessed a mass uprising of women creating their own space and asserting their own humanity. In doing so, they have added a new dimension to the history of carnivalesque and ritualesque public performances.

Works Cited

Alford, Violet. 1959. Rough Music or Charivari. *Folklore* 70(4):505–18.

Austin, J. L. 1968. *How to Do Things with Words*. Oxford: Clarendon.

Bakhtin, Mikhail. 1968. *Rabelais and His World*. Cambridge, MA: MIT Press.

Barber, Lucy G. 2004. *Marching on Washington: The Forging of an American Political Tradition*. Berkeley: University of California Press.

Beik, William. 2007. The Violence of the French Crowd from Charivari to Revolution. *Past and Present* 197(1):75–110.

Butler, Judith. 2015. *Notes toward a Performative Theory of Assembly*. Cambridge: Harvard University Press.

Cho, Sumi, Kimberley Williams Crenshaw, and Leslie McCall. 2013. Toward a Field of Intersectionality Studies: Theory, Applications, and Praxis. *Signs: Journal of Women in Culture and Society* 38(4):785–810.

Currans, Elizabeth. 2017. *Marching Dykes, Liberated Sluts and Concerned Mothers: Women Transforming Public Space*. Urbana: University of Illinois Press.

Davis, Natalie Zemon. 1975. *Society and Culture in Early Modern France*. Stanford, CA: Stanford University Press.

Greenhill, Pauline. 2010. *Make the Night Hideous: Four French-Canadian Charivaris, 1881–1940*. Toronto: University of Toronto Press.

Jarvis, Katie. 2019. *Politics in the Marketplace: Work, Gender, and Citizenship in Revolutionary France*. New York: Oxford University Press.

Mansfield, Alina. 2017. Discussant comments. "Pussywhipped" panel. American Folklore Society Annual Meeting, Minneapolis, Minnesota.

Santino, Jack. 2017. "From Carnivalesque to Ritualesque: Public Ritual and the Theater of the Street." In *Public Performances: Studies in the Carnivalesque and Ritualesque*, edited by Jack Santino, 3–15. Logan: Utah State University Press.

Thompson, E. P. 1971. "The Moral Economy of the English Crowd in the Eighteenth Century." *Past and Present* 50:76–136.

Thompson, E. P. 1991. *Customs in Common: Studies in Traditional Popular Culture*. New York: New Press.

THESE PUSSIES GRAB BACK

PROTESTING AT THE 2017 PORTLAND
WOMEN'S MARCH

Rachelle H. Saltzman

At the 2017 Women's March in Portland, Oregon, over 100,000 women and their allies of all ages and genders showed up for a festive public display event to protest the 2016 US presidential election. All the traditional features of spectacle were there: chants, rhyming slogans, costumes, and noisemaking. Puns and parody ruled on the handmade signs, which conflated issues from the most mundane (tooth decay) to the most politically urgent, such as DAPL (Dakota Access Pipeline) and Black Lives Matter. While there was a palpable fear for the future, there was also exhilaration amidst the sea of (mostly pink) pussy hats. For hours, even in the pouring January rain, participants marched, sang, and insisted loudly that "this is what democracy looks like!"

Clearly, this was not politics as usual, which generally and especially during presidential campaigns, has more than a passing acquaintance with symbolic display, as folklorist Susan Davis has noted in *Parades and Power* (1986), and historian David Glassberg in *American Historical Pageantry* (1990). But these marches were qualitatively different from any in recent years and harked

back to earlier times, to the founding of this nation (Thompson 1992), in spirit if not in content. The march signs were loaded with symbols that mocked, censured, quoted, inverted original meanings, and insisted that women, Blacks, Native Americans, Latinos, LGBTQ people, and even young girls (and boys) had a stake in the polity and a right to be counted. While there was some dissent during the planning stages regarding the inclusion or exclusion of certain topics, those disputes were nowhere in sight during the march that I experienced in Portland, Oregon.

My perspective on the 2017 Women's March is personal, political, and folkloristic. Each became integrally related to the other as the event unfolded and in the months that followed. This chapter starts with a rite of passage, which occurred, coincidentally, the day before the march and forever tied the personal to the political

for my family and me. What piqued my scholarly interest in the march itself were the verbal artistry that the homemade signs displayed and the symbolic meaning of such public displays. As the march progressed, I realized that it was indeed a spectacular example of the carnivalesque, of charivari in a political context.

The Women's March protested a narrow definition of national identity in response to the GOP's campaign of exclusivity. It was an unprecedented response to an unprecedentedly divisive campaign and election. But for me and my Jewish Cambodian American family, the focus was also tied up in my daughter's Certificate of Citizenship ceremony the day before, on inauguration day. My daughter, who was born in Cambodia, came to the US in 1999 and has been an American citizen since February 27, 2001. On that date, the Child Citizenship Act of 2000 made it possible for adopted children of American citizens to acquire American citizenship automatically upon the finalization of the adoption. Those who adopted their children afterward received a Certificate of Citizenship in the mail—another step in the process. For those who were under eighteen at the time the law took effect, citizenship was automatic; the CoC itself, the not-inexpensive proof, was not. But it wasn't really necessary—until the past few years and with the overt rise of racism and increasingly bureaucratic requirements for our foreign-born children. Instead of spending hundreds of dollars on a CoC, many of us in the foreign adoption community applied for US passports for our children—clear and

incontrovertible proof of citizenship, or so we thought. Yet although the passport (issued by the Department of State) has long been the gold standard for proving American citizenship, some US colleges and universities as well as state driver's license bureaus are no longer accepting it as such, requiring instead the CoC (issued by US Citizenship and Immigration Services), which now costs over $1,000.

I'd been defiant about refusing to get a Certificate of Citizenship for my daughter, until 2016, when even US senators advised their constituents of the prudence of getting one. Grumbling all the while, I filled out yet another batch of federal forms, assembled copies of a multitude of documents, and sent in my check for $550 (the price was set to double in December 2016). We received confirmation in due time and were given our appointment for the citizenship interview and ceremony to take place in Portland, Oregon, on January 20, 2017. That this was also to be the day of the presidential inauguration did not cross my mind, since we received our date well before the fateful election.

The ironies of the ceremony were many—swearing allegiance to the US government, promising to serve in the military, and viewing canned films filled with smiling nonwhite new citizens celebrating their new status as symbolized by montages of diverse faces at Ellis Island. But the reason that I bring the Certificate of Citizenship process into this discussion of the Women's March is not only because of the coincidence of timing for my daughter's forced rite of passage but also because the conflation of the

two experiences created a different meaning for me and for my family. Instead of being a pro forma, bureaucratic requirement, the process became a defiant act, a way of asserting with incontrovertible proof that my child, now a young woman, is a US citizen—despite all who would deny her and so many others that status because of their curious notion of what it means to be American.

Lest there be any doubt, the implicit definition of "American" is white, male, and Christian, dating from the time of John Winthrop's 1630 declaration of the Massachusetts Bay Colony as a "City upon a Hill" to the more recent neo-Nazi and KKK parades and demonstrations asserting the same, particularly the odious and puzzling "Jews will not replace us" chant at the right-wing 2017 University of Virginia march, protest, and vehicular-homicide incident. That immigrants, refugees, and children of foreign lands can become Americans does not make them white, Christian, or male. Instead, the citizenship process transforms not merely the non-American into an American but America itself into a multicultural, ever-expansive, always immanent, and ever-changing identity.

Despite my cynicism, I have to admit that the ceremony was moving, as was the Women's March the following day. We celebrated the former, as much a ritual of status confirmation as my daughter's bat mitzvah six years earlier, at lunch with Jill, an old friend from Iowa. Jill, born on the Fourth of July and a self-confessed Yankee Doodle girl herself, brought the party and gifted my daughter with all sorts of

Americana—a flag, hair band, Statue of Liberty pointer, and more. It was a festive and fun afternoon that calmed our post-ceremony jitters.

Our Midwest in the Northwest weekend continued at the home of friends who had recently relocated from Madison, Wisconsin, to Portland, Oregon. We recounted the citizenship ceremony experience, showed photos, and warmed ourselves by their fire. The next day we all hopped on public transportation and joined friends at a pre-march brunch at a Portland restaurant featuring the usual array of gluten-free, locally sourced options. We also acquired laminated protest signs and fortified ourselves for a long, chilly, and rainy day on the streets of Portland. Expecting to be surrounded by about 25,000 people, we instead experienced the crush of over 100,000. It was both exhilarating and a bit terrifying, especially as the crowd gathered, grew, and became increasingly claustrophobic as we waited for the speakers to arrive and begin speaking.

As we approached the gathering area along the Portland riverfront park area, we witnessed several subgroups preparing for the day—families, young people, a pagan circle, and groups of older women. Signs were omnipresent, colorful, and creative. My favorites were the ones with complex puns and strong graphics. This being Portland, there was also an array of people in elaborate dress, some costumes but others an extension of the usual creative adornment that defines the fashion scene in Oregon's Willamette Valley, from Portland to Eugene.

The pussy hat itself became the central symbol of and for protestors, and the hats

represented a more active form of inclusion through creative handwork (see Eleuterio's chapter, this volume). They were handmade, knitted, crocheted, or sewn. Free patterns proliferated online, and various organizations offered hats gratis. Friends, mothers, and daughters made them and gifted them to one another—a traditional way of affirming ties and creating new connections with this new, albeit contested, symbol of female and political identity (see Kaleba 2017). Folklorist, dear friend, and fellow American Folklore Society Women's Section member Erika Brady crocheted mine and my daughter's in honor of Eva's citizenship ceremony; Erika worked feverishly and generously sent them via express mail to arrive in time. The hats, ours and everyone else's, were fun, hopeful, and defiant—decidedly *not* about the inevitable female acquiescence that Trump's usage

of the term "pussy" implied in the *Access Hollywood* video.[1] By owning the term, women took back their power and reversed the oppression and disdain of women that its use symbolized.

From my perspective as a public folklorist, the march, especially the opening ceremonies, could have used some event planning technical assistance—360-degree public-address system speakers, more visible port-a-potty signs, and some kind of schedule. Thousands of us waited for over an hour, standing on wetter and wetter ground, water seeping into shoes and trickling down from our pussy hats to our hair and eyeglasses. Our raincoats became increasingly sopping—they really weren't meant for standing in place for hours in a constant drizzle. Eventually the incomprehensible speaking started, some equally sound-impaired singing happened, and more speaking; pleading chants

to start punctuated the program with cries of "Let us march!" Finally, there was movement.

Once we got started, there was some confusion as to where we were headed, but that soon resolved. Various voices in the crowd started up call-and-response chants, the most common being "Tell me what democracy looks like? This is what democracy looks like!" As we walked along, there were half-hearted attempts to sing some protest songs, with most marchers not really knowing the words. At one point someone passed around half-sheets of paper with printed protest chants, which had some traction. One of the more exciting moments occurred when we passed by several overpasses and parking garages filled with crowds; they chanted back to us, unfurled banners, and waved to those of us marching.

On the whole I found participating in this public display to be uncomfortable, both physically and emotionally. I'm much more an observer than a participant, but my husband and I wanted our daughter, just turned eighteen, to experience this very American form of political participation—a more expansive rite of passage into adulthood. It was very moving to be with her for this experience, but she's even more of an observer than I am, and her political awareness was just awakening. The election results were shocking and frightening to her, and I later found out that she spent much of the night of November 8, 2016, sobbing as she watched the returns on her laptop in her bedroom. I had a similar reaction, and I had hopes that participating in the Women's

March might restore some sense of comfort and security in this country.

For my husband and our friends, who had all participated in civil rights and antiwar protest marches decades ago—and our Wisconsin colleagues more recently in Madison during recall demonstrations aimed against Governor Scott Walker—the singing, chanting, marching, and waving signs felt familiar, even normal. Yet even they commented on the need for written call-and-response slogans instead of the purely oral ones that they'd previously experienced; it was as if participants didn't quite have or recognize the script for a protest march. I didn't feel quite a part of the process myself until we pulled out of the crowd, and I really started taking pictures. Actively documenting the signs, outfits, and chants was what finally affirmed my more familiar role—as event ethnographer.

The signs, most handmade, were particularly creative and marked the most festive, multilayered, and multivocal aspects of the march. A few reflected the sometimes-speechless reaction to the turn of events. Many commented on Trump's notorious thin skin, sexually abusive behavior, and physical traits indicative of his character traits. Others used his quotes or speech pattern to mock the man, as political parades (Davis 1986) and carnivalesque events (Darnton 1984; Saltzman 1995; Santino 2016; Robles 2019; Thompson 1992) are wont to do. Parodic slogans excoriated perceived political and moral wrongdoing: hypocrisy, racism, xenophobia, and the right-wing determination to strip women, people of color, immigrants, and the poor of

their humanity—to dehumanize them and make them into alien others (Goffman 1963). Yet they were also insistently positive and inclusive—for women's rights, environmental protection, Native rights, Black Lives, humane values, creativity, and intelligence— attesting to the creative power of bricolage (Lévi-Strauss 1963) and multivocality that characterizes festivals (Bakhtin 1968).

As in many public display events (Abrahams 1981), especially those tilting at the power structure, individual participants became bricoleurs as they drew from a range of popular culture, political issues, newsworthy topics, and historical key symbols to cocreate a festive procession (Davis 1986; Saltzman 2012). The various signs employed all sorts of devices—puns, parodies, alliteration, assonance, repetition, caricature, exaggeration, metaphor, and other forms of verbal and visual artistry—to call attention to

the gross violations of social norms and democratic values. This particular style of vernacular art plays well into the multivocality that typifies the carnivalesque and was most apparent on the handmade signs, many of which were also memes. Their "logic," that of puns, parody, and satire, comes from the multiple layers of meanings encoded in the very economical number of words sometimes layered onto a visual. They are meaningful only if one understands the full context, often historical and contemporary.[2]

Quotes from Trump as well as those from a panoply of famously progressive people, including Desmond Tutu, Susan B. Anthony, Hillary Rodham Clinton, and John Lennon, signified—without being explicit—the difference between the president's America and that of the sign bearers. References to contemporary films and songs, the Bible, and the US Constitution

and Declaration of Independence functioned similarly—defining our nation as we wanted it to be. Many referenced and conflated topical issues: Trump's vaunted wall between the US and Mexico, the Dakota Access Pipeline, Black Lives Matter, and Russian president Putin's election interference—all censured deviations from preferred social norms. Signs often combined pop culture, film, and television references to women's rights, which made for even more puns, e.g., "Hear me Roar,"[3] "Orange is the New Black,"[4] and "A woman's place is in the resistance."[5] Just as the participants represented a diversity of faces, genders, and ages, so did signs in different languages (Arabic, Spanish, and Hebrew, as well as English)—all speaking to the multivocal, multicultural protest against this regime.

As I was writing the conference version of this chapter, I happened to be reading *Summerland*, Michael Chabon's coming-of-age novel about industrial pollution (2002). The behind-the-scenes main character is Coyote—the infamous trickster in many Native American narratives; Coyote is not only a trickster but the destroyer—and also the giver—of life. His short attention span, his focus on disruption and destruction, and his ego eventually enable the young hero and his band of misfits to trick the trickster, right their world, and end the chaos. As I was reading the novel, Donald Trump was incessantly tweeting his usual shocking comments—about the hurricanes that ravaged Texas, Florida, and Puerto Rico; about North Korea's leader and total destruction; and about the 2017 mass shooting massacre at a country

music concert in Las Vegas. Indeed, on any given day, he's tweeting or doing something comparably or even more outrageous—it's hard to keep up. My conflation of these two realities led me to the recognition that Trump's role was that of a certain kind of trickster—a disrupter and destroyer. At the same time, I was looking backward to 2016, to a playful yet meaningful ceremony in which I had participated. At the American Folklore Society's Women's Croning[6] in Miami, folklorist Jack Santino portrayed Trump exactly this way—as trickster, mocking and disrupting the proceedings, which eventually cast him aside in favor of a new order and the eventual triumph of the crones—at least for this rite of passage if not yet in American society.

Yet, as Jack commented more recently, "I wonder if there is a distinction to be made between trickster as cultural outlaw and trickster in the Native American sense of cosmic force representing chaos?" (personal communication 2019). As he noted, we scholars and even the general public have this general idea of a trickster as a sort of cultural outlaw, a perspective that comes from Native American societies (Radin 1972) as well as from Greek, Hindu, Buddhist, and others that paint tricksters as cosmic forces—dangerous and "always threatening to overwhelm civilized order (culture) with uncontrollable chaos (nature)." Yet Trump's trickster is not like traditional Native American figures such as Raven, Crow, Coyote, or even like the Hindu Shiva, who all incorporate both sacred and profane aspects of life. There is nothing sacred about Trump—he is all profanity, the quintessential outlaw, which seems to be what Trump likes to promote about himself and what his followers seem to appreciate about him. He is the destroyer who leaves nothing good in his wake—unlike those folk tricksters who embody the creative immanent energy that births new worlds.

Carnivalesque events like the 2017 women's marches create the possibility of ritualesque moments (Santino 2017), when the so-called time-out-of-time perception of *communitas* and flow to which scholars of ritual and festival refer occurs (Abrahams 1987; Babcock 1984; Davis 1986; Geertz 1973; Stoeltje 1992; Turner 1982, 2012). I would argue that when I have experienced them in my own life (usually during a rite of passage), those moments are, instead, "time *in* time." They are the *most* real perceptions we can have about how society could be. I've also noticed this phenomenon when I've interviewed

Jack Santino wearing a Trump mask at the 2016 American Folklore Society Women's Section Croning. Photo by Nick Bocher, with permission of Nick Bocher.

people about their experiences of war or other traumatic periods. We carry the deep and intense realness of those moments back into the everyday to "reconstruct our identities, relationships, and histories" (Jack Santino, personal communication 2019), to do the work of ritual transformation in ways that enable structural change.

But sometimes, despite the intensity of a particular historical moment, the way forward is not always clear in the immediate aftermath. Despite the strong organization of the Women's March, the "script" for protest was hazy, and *communitas* was somehow elusive amidst the cheerful hats, colorful costumes, awkward chanting, and waving signs. In the days, weeks, and months that followed, those feelings of oneness and plans for future action did emerge on social media, in the postings of narratives and photos as March participants exchanged memories and then started to talk about changes and what should come next. Those exchanges, which included shared stories of successes, setbacks, traumas, tears, and affirmations, were and are particularly evident in the "secret [Facebook] group" Pantsuit Nation, to which Hillary Rodham Clinton referred in her concession speech. That virtual coming together, among nearly four million friends and strangers, which transformed into what felt and feels like an endless series of petitions, phone calls, and marches, has instead become a longer-lasting and more hospitable home for generative social change.

As a folklorist I am fascinated by the conflation of traditional, performative, folkloric behavior when people employ it for political

purposes (Saltzman 1994, 1995, 2012). What attracted me about the Women's March was how it reflected the spirit of charivari, of rough music, that communal folk spirit and insistence on justice and right order that arises when legal means of redress do not work (Alford 1959; Beik 2007; Darnton 1984; Hay et al. 1975; Hobsbawm and Ranger 1975; MacAloon 1984;; Saltzman 2012; Tuleja 1997; Turner 1973). Rough music makes audience members into performers to counter, critique, and censure—to present an alternative vision (Smith and Saltzman 1995). And the Women's March did just that—it was a response and a protest—an affirmation of a more expansive notion of what it is to be American as well as a boisterous and joyful reclaiming of the power to define what it is to be a US citizen. Chants, songs, and even the clang of a pot and wooden spoon complemented the nasty women and pussy protest signs that defiantly called out sexual harassment, sex abuse, and more.

Thus, the charivari that emerged into full-blown performance during the Women's Marches of 2017 may have been playful, but it was not about fun; this was serious play. Images of vaginas, even of the mythical vagina dentata (Otero 1996), were on display—and their meaning was clear: "these pussies grab back."[7] When our world has been turned upside down, we grasp for ways to recreate some semblance of right order. Declarations of women's rights, human rights, dykes for choice, Black Lives Matter, and pussy power represent that right order, insisting, just as Elizabeth Warren "persisted" (Wang 2017), that "we are not ovary-acting." *We* are making change.

Notes

Photos in this chapter were taken by Rachelle H. Saltzman unless otherwise noted.

1. In the now-infamous *Access Hollywood* video from 2005, Trump told Billy Bush about his seduction attempt with a married woman and declared, "I don't even wait. And when you're a star, they let you do it. You can do anything. Grab them by the pussy. You can do anything."

The Wikipedia entry about this video quotes Nancy O'Dell, the married woman in question:

"Politics aside, I'm saddened that these comments still exist in our society at all. When I heard the comments yesterday, it was disappointing to hear such objectification of women. The conversation needs to change because no female, no person, should be the subject of such crass comments, whether or not cameras are rolling. Everyone deserves respect no matter the setting or gender. As a woman who has worked very hard to establish her career, and as a mom, I feel I must speak out with the hope that as a society we will always strive to be better."

2. Memes, like photocopy lore, allow us to comment anonymously (whoever claimed to create a photocopy joke—or meme?). We can use them in the same way we pass around aural jokes. We have the ability to say something profound with humor, sometimes with some kind of pun involved (Marsh 2015; Michael 1995). One-liners or quips--what I've called collapsed narratives—make sense only because one knows the backstory, the context of the joke or quip; the combination creates the meaning (Saltzman 2012:136–54).

3. This sign refers to popular singer Katy Perry's 2013 feminist coming-of-age song "Roar," which itself references Helen Reddy's 1971 feminist anthem "I Am Woman."

4. "Orange Is the New Black" is a Netflix television series about women in prison, based on Piper Kerman's book by the same name. The pun is a pointed reference to Trump's purported criminal behavior, especially those related to his self-described sexual abuse of women, a theme that dogged his campaign. And it further parodies the series' tongue-in-cheek fashion statement implicit in the Netflix series' title with Trump's aggrandizing of his social position.

5. This meme ("A Woman's Place Is in the Resistance") refers to the 2016 "Rogue One: A Star Wars Story" and feminist actor Carrie Fisher's portrayal of Princess Leia's fierce resistance leadership; the signs incorporated the meme overlaying a picture of Fisher's Princess Leia wielding an imperial blaster weapon. This image also conflated Fisher's tragic and then-recent death with her seeming ability to overcome impossible odds to become one of the faces of the 2017 Women's March.

6. The AFS Women's Section has long held a raucous croning ceremony for its members when they reach the age of fifty. This highly performative rite of passage includes numerous popular culture references, some kind of battle, the triumph of the crones, and a specific though variable ceremony to welcome the

newly croned into the motherhood of wise women. We repossessed the term crone and imbued it, as did the creators and wearers of pussy hats, with positive connotations in direct contrast to popular culture's mostly negative meanings.

7. Kim Boekbinder's 2016 song "Pussy Grabs Back" was inspired by *Feminist Fight Club* author Jessica Bennett's image of a snarling cat head atop a woman's body. The song, a direct response to Trump's braggadocio, declares, "We're not daughters, not wives / We're humans with lives / On November 8th / We're gonna rock it." See Andrea Glass's chapter for more on this topic and Puglise 2016.

Works Cited

Abrahams, Roger D. 1981. Shouting Match at the Border: The Folklore of Display Events. In *"And Other Neighborly Names": Social Process and Culture Image in Texas Folklore*, edited by Richard Bauman and Roger D. Abrahams, 303–21. Austin: University of Texas Press.

Abrahams, Roger D. 1987. An American Vocabulary of Celebrations. In *Time Out of Time: Essays on the Festival*, edited by Alessandro Falassi, 173–82. Albuquerque: University of New Mexico Press.

Alford, Violet. 1959. Rough Music or Charivari. *Folklore* 70(4):505–518.

Babcock, Barbara. 1984. Arrange Me into Disorder. In *Dramas, Rites, Spectacles and Festivals: Rehearsals towards a Theory of Cultural Performance*, edited by John MacAloon, 1–20. Philadelphia: Institute for the Study of Human Issues.

Bakhtin, Mikhail. 1968. *Rabelais and His World*. Cambridge: MIT Press.

Beik, William. 2007. The Violence of the French Crowd from Charivari to Revolution. *Past and Present* 197(1):75–110.

Chabon, Michael. 2002. *Summerland*. New York: HarperCollins Publishers.

Darnton, Robert. 1984. *The Great Cat Massacre*. New York: Basic Books.

Davis, Susan. 1986. *Parades and Power*. Philadelphia: University of Pennsylvania Press.

Geertz, Clifford. 1973. *The Interpretation of Cultures*. New York: Basic Books.

Glassberg, David. 1990. *American Historical Pageantry*. Chapel Hill: University of North Carolina Press.

Goffman, Erving. 1963. *Stigma: Notes on the Management of a Spoiled Identity*. London: Penguin.

Hay, Douglas, Peter Linebaugh, John G. Rule, E. P. Thompson, and Cal Winslow. 1975. *Albion's Fatal Tree*. New York: Pantheon Books.

Hobsbawm, Eric, and George Rudé, eds. 1975. *Captain Swing*. London: W. W. Norton.

Kaleba, Kerry. 2017. The Pussy Hat Project. Annual Meeting, American Folklore Society. MS.

Lévi-Strauss, Claude. 1962. *The Savage Mind*. London: University of Chicago Press.

MacAloon, John, ed. 1984. *Rites, Dramas, Festival, Spectacle: Rehearsals Towards a Theory of Cultural Performance*. Philadelphia: Institute for the Study of Human Issues.

Marsh, Moira. 2015. *Practically Joking*. Logan: Utah State University Press.

Michael, Nancy. 1995. Censure of a Photocopylore Display. *Journal of Folklore Research* (special issue) 32(2):137–54.

Otero, Solimar. 1996. "Fearing Our Mothers": An Overview of the Psychoanalytic Theories concerning the Vagina Dentata Motif F547.1.1. *American Journal of Psychoanalysis* 56(269):269–88. https://doi.org/10.1007/BF02742415.

Puglise, Nicole. 2016. "Pussy Grabs Back" Becomes Rallying Cry for Female Rage against Trump. *Guardian*, October 10. https://www.theguardian.com/us-news/2016/oct/10/donald-trump-pussy-grabs-back-meme-women-twitter.

Radin, Paul. 1972. *The Trickster: A Study in American Indian Mythology*. New York: Schocken Books.

Robles, Frances. 2019. Protests Are Still Erupting in Puerto Rico: This Time, It's over Wanda Vazquez as Governor. *New York Times*. July 29. https://www.nytimes.com/2019/07/29/us/puerto-rico-march-vazquez-rossello.html.

Saltzman, Rachelle H. 1994. Calico Indians and Pistol Pills: Historical Symbols and Political Action. *New York Folklore* 20(3–4):1–18.

Saltzman, Rachelle H. 1995. 'This Buzz Is For You': Popular Responses to the Ted Bundy Execution. *Journal of Folklore Research* (Special Issue) 32(2):101–20.

Saltzman, Rachelle H. 2012. *A Lark for the Sake of Their Country: The 1926 General Strike in Folklore and Memory*. Manchester: Manchester University Press.

Santino, Jack. 2017. "From Carnivalesque to Ritualesque: Public Ritual and the Theater of the Street." In *Public Performances: Studies in the Carnivalesque and Ritualesque*, edited by Jack Santino, 3–15. Logan: Utah State University Press.

Smith, Moira, and Rachelle H Saltzman. 1995. Arbiters of Taste: Censuring/Censoring Discourse. *Journal of Folklore Research* (special issue) 32(2):85–100.

Stoeltje, Beverly. 1992. Festival. In *Folklore, Cultural Performances, and Popular Entertainments*, edited by Richard Bauman, 261–71. New York: Oxford University Press.

Thompson, E. P. 1992. *Customs in Common*. New York: New Press.

Tuleja, Tad, ed. 1997. *Usable Expressions: Traditions and Group Expressions in North America*. Logan: Utah State University Press.

Turner, Edith. 2012. *Communitas: The Anthropology of Collective Joy*. Palgrave Macmillan.

Turner, Victor. 1973. *Dramas, Fields, and Metaphors*. Ithaca: Cornell University Press.

Turner, Victor. 1982. *The Ritual Process*. Ithaca: Cornell Paperbacks.

Wang, Amy. 2017. "Nevertheless, She Persisted" Becomes New Battle Cry after McConnell Silences Elizabeth Warren. *Washington Post*, February 8. https://www.washingtonpost.com/news/the-fix/wp/2017/02/08/nevertheless-she

-persisted-becomes-new-battle-cry-after-mcconnell-silences-elizabeth
-warren/?noredirect=on&utm_term=.e9ob2f3ec626.
Wikipedia. 2019. Donald Trump Access Hollywood Tape. https://en.wikipedia
.org/wiki/Donald_Trump_Access_Hollywood_tape_[modified_Monday,
August 26, 2019, 9:42:52 AM].

PUSSY HATS

COMMON GROUND AT THE CHICAGO WOMEN'S MARCH

Susan Eleuterio

In response to President Donald Trump's crude, recorded comments about grabbing women by their genitals, pussy hats emerged as a symbol of resistance at the January 21, 2017, Chicago Women's March. Whether knitted, made from felt, or crocheted, the small, primarily pink hats served as material representation of the Chicago March motto: "connected, protected, and activated." The women (and men) of all ages who wore the hats displayed unified opposition to the stated goals of the Trump administration and, at the same time, uniquely individual expressions. As time has gone on, their owners have continued to use the hats to reappropriate and recontextualize their meaning, from insulting term into symbol of power. An activist who prefers to remain anonymous sent me a letter in which she described the hat she wore:

> I knitted a total of 8 Pussy Hats. I knitted three before the 2017 Women's March Chicago: I wore one and passed out two that morning to a couple of other women attending. I passed out the remaining five at various protests in the months that followed. The photo that I sent to you was taken at "Not My President's Day" in

February 2017. I've worn it multiple times in the last couple of years—but only to protests where I feel safe and I know others will also be wearing them. (Anonymous, letter to author, 2019)

Folklorist Linda Pershing, whose study of fabric arts in her work on women who advocate for peace, points out, "In political needlework, women have acknowledged and manipulated the conceptual association of the fabric arts with femininity, domesticity and compliance with socially prescribed gender roles. They have learned to use this to their advantage in order to convey their views through a medium that has been acceptable to the general society and readily accessible to women" (Pershing 1996:54).

In Chicago, and at other marches around the country and the world, pussy hats functioned as symbols of protest and unity against perceived threats not only to women's rights but also to those of immigrants, LGBTQ individuals, and people of color. The hats, along with the process of creating and sharing them, became contemporary badges of expression and community, a process that has continued over several years. Wearing them to a variety of events has become a ritualized expression for many Chicago-area women. As folklorist Jack Santino notes, "ritual . . . has a direct and ongoing effect on everyday life . . . changes wrought by ritual are carried into the world and can be incorporated into everyday life as part of a new status quo" (Santino 2011:68).

As a marcher and volunteer marshal for the march, I found myself not only wearing a hat but also becoming interested in how other women decided to wear them. What follows highlights an eclectic sampling of how different women have created, worn, and repurposed the pussy hats and other head covers from the 2017 Chicago Women's March. Included are vignettes from several women who marched in Chicago or live in the region, which includes the six-county Chicago metropolitan area and northwest Indiana. In her volume on Mexican minorities, *México's Nobodies*, Christine Arce notes "there is an intimate link—that is not metaphoric—between art, crafting textiles, spirituality, community, and knowledge" (Arce 2017:22). Those of us who wore pussy hats at the march, made and shared them in the days leading up to the event, and wore them on subsequent occasions, cocreated similarly strong and intimate connections.

Jayna Zweiman and Krista Suh originated the idea of making pussy hats for the DC women's march. The *Huffington Post's* Catherine Pearson noted that Zweiman and Suh regarded the goals of sharing and establishing community as central to the Pussyhat Project from the beginning.

> Suh and Zweiman don't have an exact sense of how many pink cat-eared hats will be at the march. Partly, it's because they're encouraging people to give hats to marchers directly if possible, although they can also be dropped off at participating knit shops across the country that will get them to the march, or shipped directly to the Pussyhat Project. But it's also because the founders say they're more concerned with creating community than in reaching any specific distribution goals. (Pearson 2017)

Truly folk artifacts, the hats were not mass produced but individually created. The process of sewing, knitting, or crocheting and then gifting the hats represents values inherent in women's traditional craft. Leslie Hauser, now a community manager at *Run for Something*, which recruits "diverse progressives" to run for office, notes:

> I attended the Women's March with my daughter and husband—my first political march in 25

Anonymous activist wearing pussy hat in front of Trump Tower, Chicago, 2017. Photo by anonymous activist.

Marchers at the 2017 Chicago Women's March. Photo by Susan Eleuterio.

years! I sewed 50+ pussy hats and shared with friends and sent most to DC. After the March, wanting to get more involved in making the world a better place, I spent six months working on Ameya Pawar's gubernatorial campaign in Volunteer onboarding. It was an awesome experience and I will stay involved in politics, just no longer in this IL governor's race. (personal communication October 2017)

To illustrate the process of community making, Hauser shared a photo of her family members wearing the hats she made; this practice centered around the giving and sharing of hats (and other material culture, such as pins). This is characteristic of many women's friendships, for such gifting to sustain community has long been part of American women's culture. Examples include exchanges of baby blankets, hats, scarves, mittens, and wedding quilts at showers, for birthdays, and on other occasions. My own grandmother, a seamstress, crocheted a blanket for me that remains one of my most treasured possessions. Educator and researcher Tracy Rogers-Tryba writes:

> I gifted my daughter her own pussy hat in early March when visiting her in Boston. I also gave a set of hats to my 11 and 13 year old nieces. We've worn our hats with pride to symbolize the rights and recognition that we deserve EQUITY. That #MeToo (movement) is real. It's prevalent in the patriarchy of higher educational institutions (my environment) and in the STEM field of architecture [her field]. We each hope and strive to make the world a more equitable and kinder place for all humans, of all "isms." Our efforts are a drop in the pond and one of many ripples, but together we are a wave of change that must move forward, never backward, using our collective strength in this universal struggle. Feminism is not something to be ashamed of but something to empower us collectively. (personal communication October 2017)

At the start of the Chicago Women's March, one of the marshals handed out homemade hats to everyone, including me. I had conflicting feelings about wearing a pussy hat: I don't like to wear hats, and I was concerned about nonrepresentational issues of race and gender that some who chose to sit out the women's marches had raised (Shamus 2018); I also do not knit or crochet. What was a surprise for me personally was how the hat provided a literal sense of "cover" as thousands of marchers ignored the police and started walking through downtown Chicago's Loop area. Receiving the hat as a gift immediately made me feel "connected and protected." Because we marshals were wearing bright yellow vests, the hat also made me feel less like a "cop" and more like a helpful participant.

Women have historically used color to express support for causes from the gold and white (and later white and purple) of suffragettes, to the pink of Planned Parenthood supporters and breast cancer survivors, to the rainbow colors of the LGBTQ

Tracy Rogers-Tryba and daughter wearing pussy hats. Photo by Tracy Rogers-Tryba.

community. As is the case with all folk material culture expressions, makers and wearers used color to express both unity and individuality. Martha Sims and Martine Stephens highlight this element of creativity in folk practice and note, "Toelken suggests that folklore possesses both 'dynamic' (changing) and 'conservative' (static) features that allow it to be adaptable yet still maintain a sense of continuity" (Sims and Stephens 2005:76–77) Thus, those who chose to don pussy hats wore a range of colors and styles; those worn at the Chicago Women's March and by activists at other events ranged in color from hot pink to red and even black. At the 2017 rally for Indiana and Kentucky's local Planned Parenthood affiliate in northwest Indiana, pink hats were prevalent, even among transgendered participants (counter to some of the media commentary about who was willing to wear pussy hats).

Chicago Women's March participants
with different colored hats, 2017.
Photo by Susan Eleuterio.

Women wore different-colored head coverings for different reasons. In the fall of 2017, I met activist Deb Quantock-McCarey at a downtown Chicago vigil for victims of the Las Vegas shooting, which also served as a rally for increased gun control legislation in Illinois. Deb participated in the DC Women's March but lives in a nearby suburb of Chicago and has kept involved with cause-based protests locally. She told me that her friend ran out of pink wool, so she made her a green and purple hat, since Deb is an active gardener and birder (the green) as well as a supporter of women's rights (the purple). She recalled, "I went on the bus to DC to stand for/support all women, but especially those who are blind, deaf/blind or living with a visual impairment (permanent loss of central vision) as I am" (personal communication 2017).

Jacqui Algee, an SEIU (Service Employees International Union) Healthcare organizer, pictured here with another volunteer marshal, trained the marshals for the Chicago march. Algee, a practicing Muslim, wore a purple headscarf to represent her affiliation with SEIU. As some commentaries about pussy hats have noted, not all women have pink vaginas; each woman made choices about headgear and other clothing to fit her personal beliefs.

Since the 2017 Women's March, pussy hats have remained a symbol of resistance to continued misogyny, not only from the Trump administration but also in American life and politics in general. For example, one group of Chicago organizers created the Pink Hat Run in the fall of 2017.

Jacqui Algee and volunteer at
Chicago Women's March, 2017.
Photo by Susan Eleuterio.

While the images posted on Facebook included what appears to be a "pussy hat," the hats sold to raise money for the event had lost their "cat" ears and were simply knitted pink hats.

The organizers of the Pink Hat Run were noticeably silent as to why the change from "pussy hat" to "pink hat." This was puzzling, since their website featured many images from the Women's March. I suspect their decision was both based on the perceived exclusion of transgender and women of color by the use of pink (although ironically, the Pussyhat Project co-founder,

Planned Parenthood rally, Merrillville,
Indiana, 2017. Photo by Betsy Hunt.

Krista Suh, is Chinese American) and with an eye, perhaps, toward not alienating the run's corporate funders.

Marchers and marshalls, Chicago Women's March, 2017. Photo by Susan Eleuterio.

For the past two years, I have kept my own hat on my dresser as a kind of shrine to activism. I wore it again when I went to the 2018 Women's March in Baltimore, where I was teaching. I've continued to be both grateful for the gift of solidarity and a bit shy about wearing it.

Since the 2017 Women's March, women have continued to wear the hats to signify community as well as resistance—to the actions and politics of the Trump administration and also to restrictions of women's and immigrants' rights. Former northwest Indiana resident Maui Thomas writes, "I went to the first woman's march, but I don't have my hat [from] when I participated in it. I wore a bright pink hat with a safety pin going to the march

Pink Hat Run website photo, 2017.

Photo by Tracy Baim.

Solidarity Against White Supremacy. The hat symbolizes that I am fighting for equality and immigrants' right to live peacefully" (personal communication n.d.). The rise of the #MeToo movement, as Tracy Rogers-Tryba notes in her description of the significance of the hats, has only increased the need for solidarity and activism among a wide range of women in the Chicago area, nationally, and internationally.

By incorporating women's expressive and traditional culture in giving gifts, making and using textile arts for the purposes of political and cultural change, and using humor and individual statements to counter sexism, racism, and other prejudices, pussy hats have become an important part of women's culture in Chicago and elsewhere. As Lou Taylor, professor of dress and textile history, writes: "cloth and clothing . . . is a powerful cultural enforcer, carrier, enhancer, transmitter and celebrator" (Taylor 2002:236). By reframing an insult as something joyous, women in Chicago and elsewhere have created an all-purpose symbol of protest that has expanded beyond the confines of the Women's March and into their lives in Trump's America.

Pink Hat Run photo, 2017. Photo by
Leni Manaa-Hoppenworth.

Works Cited

Arce, Christine. 2017. *México's Nobodies: The Cultural Legacy of the Soldadera
    and Afro-Mexican Women*. Albany: State University of New York Press.
Farenthold, David. 2016. Trump Recorded Having Extremely Lewd Conversa-
    tion about Women in 2005. *Washington Post*, October 8. https://www
    .washingtonpost.com/politics/trump-recorded-having-extremely-lewd
    -conversation-about-women-in-2005/2016/10/07/3b9ce776–8cb4–11e6-bf8a
    -3d26847eeed4_story.html?noredirect=on&utm_term=.3739201d67e8.
Pearson, Catherine. 2017. Thousands Are Knitting Pussy Hats for the Women's
    March on Washington. *Huffington Post*, January 3. https://www
    .huffingtonpost.com/entry/thousands-are-knitting-pussy-hats-for-the
    -womens-march-on-washington_us_586bb22ee4b0d9a5945c636a.
Pershing, Linda. 1996. *The Ribbon around the Pentagon: Peace by
    Piecemakers*. Knoxville: University of Tennessee Press.
Santino. Jack. 2011. The Carnivalesque and the Ritualesque. *Journal of American
    Folklore*, 124(491):61–73.

Shamus, Kristen Jordan. 2018. Pussyhats: The Reason Feminists Are Ditching
    Them. *Detroit Free Press*, January 1. https://www.freep.com/story/news
    /2018/01/10/pink-pussyhats-feminists-hats-womens-march/1013630001/.
    Accessed October 18, 2018.
Sims, Martha, and Stephens, Martine. 2005. *Living Folklore; An Introduction to
    the Study of People and Their Traditions*. Logan: Utah State University Press.
Taylor, Lou. 2002. *The Study of Dress History*. London: Manchester University Press.

POSTCARDS, PUSSY HATS, AND PROTEST PINS

DOCUMENTING THE FOLKLORE OF FEMINIST RESISTANCE AT MIO STUDIO IN LANCASTER

Andrea Glass

On the surface, the City of Lancaster, Pennsylvania, can serve as a case study for a host of different demographic observations in the Trump era. In 2016, the *New York Post* questioned whether the City of Lancaster could perhaps be the new Brooklyn, and the *New York Times*, *New York Daily News*, and *Philadelphia Magazine* all noted the city's ever-evolving food scene and arts and cultural opportunities. By contrast, Lancaster County as a whole has a strong conservative majority, a rich agricultural heritage, and a focus on religious traditions. The 2016 election only accentuated the differences between the City of Lancaster and the county at large and the urban-rural divide that had become increasingly more apparent across the United States. My research is concerned with the acts of feminist resistance at Mio Studio, which occurred within this partisan and polarized landscape.

In this chapter, I am largely concerned with documenting and better understanding how certain acts of resistance are moving

feminist and queer theory from an academic realm into the public sphere. Rhetorical patterns, folk art, and material culture are often the evidentiary markers of that transition from ideology to practice and one place in particular, Mio Studio, was effective in using contemporary craft to engage in queer feminist protest. Mio Studio was one of the most visible supporters of local and national Democratic candidates during the 2016 election season. Mio Studio is an LGBT-owned, Latinx-owned, and woman-owned art gallery at the intersection of two busy and highly visible streets in downtown Lancaster.[1] The owners, Erica Millner and her wife, Mai Orama Muniz, started making jewelry nineteen years ago in Puerto Rico. They are known for their use of exotic woods and metals, as well as their ability to reuse local materials in the pieces that they produce. Their work has been featured in numerous shows and festivals, most notably the Smithsonian's Craft Show.[2] In April of 2017, the Pennsylvania Guild of Craftsmen recognized the couple as master craftsmen.

Erica and Mai are familiar downtown faces. They have been involved in a wide variety of local initiatives, community organizations, and area action groups. Erica has coordinated Lancaster's Pride festival in the past. In 2011, President Barack Obama invited the duo to the White House for a reception to acknowledge their commitment to LGBTQ+ causes. It was through the LGBT Center of Central Pennsylvania that I had first encountered Erica and Mai. At the time I was a board member for the center and a committee member for their history project. In September of 2016, I joined the gallery as an artist-in-residence to work on my research and to display corresponding photography projects.

I had no intentions of writing formally about Erica and Mai or their artistic efforts at Mio Studio. Shortly after I arrived, however, patterns started to emerge at the gallery that I could not ignore. In the fall of 2016, Mio became both a safe space for the LGBTQ+ community and a site for storytelling and cultural exchange before, during, and after the presidential election. While Erica and Mai have a history of participating in politics and community activism, the 2016 election marked the first time they used their jewelry to make a much larger public political statement.

That jewelry represents a significant grassroots example at the intersection of contemporary craft, rhetoric, and resistance. What started as simple social action projects at Mio Studio evolved into planned and unplanned opportunities at the gallery for community members to exchange stories of protest, seek counseling and advice, and meet likeminded others. A distinct expressive culture and rhetorical patterns emerged on jewelry and clothing as well as on posters and window displays. A new material culture of resistance simultaneously developed that was both part of larger national trends and uniquely local. Exchanging stories about area marches, visits to the offices of local elected officials, and positive and negative community experiences allowed participants to heal, feel empowered, and receive direction for future action. Mio Studio became a safe and intersectional space, one for all ages—a trusted source of information for community organizing efforts, upcoming events, and resources and opportunities.

On October 21, 2016, Erica and Mai released their first "resistance jewelry," quarter-sized aluminum charms on simple leather cord necklaces with slogans such as "Nasty Woman," "Pussy Grabs Back," and "Bad Hombre." The charms both reacted to and engaged in partisan discourse. "Pussy Grabs Back" was a feminist rhetorical response to the 2005 tape of Donald Trump that surfaced in early October of 2016. On the tape, Trump could be heard boasting to Billy Bush on the set of *Days of Our Lives* about being able to grab women by the pussy because of his celebrity status. Less than two weeks later, Trump referred to Clinton as "such a nasty woman" during the final presidential debate at the University of Nevada, Las Vegas. He also famously uttered, "We have some bad hombres here and we're going to get 'em out," during that same debate. While those slogans all had larger national significance—trending online and appearing on mass-produced apparel—Erica and Mai's simple hand-forged pieces imbued those slogans with renewed significance within the local community.

Initially, there was no charge for the charms, an important point. Mio Studio's Facebook and Instagram pages promoted the first charms; for Erica, they were a way to reinforce solidarity and give back to their community. The initial demand was overwhelming. Less than two weeks after the project's launch, Erica had to post a message on social media to alert her customers and friends about their limited availability. In two weeks Erica had made and given away 150 tags. The charms continued to be available after November 4, but for a modest cost.

Erica's message also referenced a podcast, 94.1 KPFA's *The Visionary Activist Show*, which had inspired the social action project. On October 13, Caroline Casey, the show's host in Berkeley, California, interviewed Eve Ensler and Bob Gough. Ensler is a playwright and activist best known for *The Vagina Monologues* and the rise of V-Day, a global movement to end violence against women and girls. Ensler spoke passionately about the need to come together as a unified movement, to look for the opportunities in the crises around us, and to make the most of this historic moment. The podcast also referenced Kim Boekbinder's protest song "Pussy Grabs Back." Erica subsequently posted the song's video on social media and used "Pussy Grabs Back" memes on Facebook. She also circulated the popular illustration for the *Feminist Fight Club* created by Jessica Bennett, Amanda Duarte, and Stella Mars.

Erica's jewelry answered Ensler's call with a concrete message and method to facilitate critical dialogue surrounding current issues and feminist concerns. The charms were physical manifestations of this cultural response—material items of resistance that were not only inspired by these larger trends but were also in conversation with them. The Lancaster community viewed Erica and Mai as authority figures and trendsetters, a fact that aided in the circulation of queer feminist rhetoric and visual culture at a local level.

The jewelry also became part of a gendered performance—inspiring customers to share in person and online the reasons that the Nasty Woman campaign resonated personally with them. Most women posted photos of themselves wearing the jewelry with messages of gratitude. One supporter wrote, "Thank you Erica and Mai for finding such a creative expression for our feelings! We love you for it!" For some, the jewelry represented their strength, beauty, and courage. One woman, Rose, posted a photo of herself wearing the "Pussy Grabs Back" necklace along with the message "feeling myself" and the hashtags #rockstar and #lovinglife. Customers described the necklaces as "kick ass" and helping to "shout anger." The pictures made a statement about not only the poster's political beliefs but also their identity.

Customers who came into Mio Studio expressed similar sentiments, and they shared their stories as they picked up their charms. Many viewed the charms as personal badges of honor that symbolized their journey, accomplishments, and struggles. A local woman in her eighties described the challenges of being a woman in Lancaster and her lifetime as a feminist activist. She entered the shop unable to utter the word "pussy" but left proudly wearing her "Pussy Grabs Back" necklace. It was also not uncommon for customers to point out and discuss the messages on their T-shirts and campaign buttons, conversations that reinforced solidarity among those present. One woman even stressed that she was putting her charm inside her Planned Parenthood tote bag. Other customers talked about those they were gifting with the charms; one woman mentioned that she was giving one to a professor of Women and Gender Studies.

Erica and Mai also created a custom pin with the Clinton campaign's logo in Mio Studio's classic metal and wood style. Proceeds from the pins' sale benefited Hillary's campaign, and the pins were a common sight at local political fundraisers. On November 3, 2016, Erica presented one of the pins to Gloria Steinem when Steinem visited the City of Lancaster to campaign for Hillary Clinton. Mai also created a miniature version of the pin and attached it to one of her signature wooden bird sculptures, which she prominently placed in the gallery windows to inform passersby of Mio Studio's support for Clinton. Customers also posted photos of the pins as well as images of themselves wearing the pins in the community. On the morning of the election, one customer, Kathlene, wrote,

> I am ready for a very early morning at my polling place with my special outfit ready to go. Plenty of Hillary swag thanks to the fabulous brooch from Erica and Mai (Mio Studio) and my "Women for H" T! Topping it all off with something white, of course, to honor the years of work of the women who sacrificed so much in the women's suffrage movement. I am ready for a morning of history!! #ImWithHer (Sullivan 2016)

Like Kathlene, Erica and Mai also wore white pantsuits and the Mio Studio brooch to their polling place. On the morning of the election, they posted their picture to their social media feeds and the popular Pantsuit Nation Facebook group.

In October of 2016, Libby Chamberlain created the Pantsuit Nation Facebook group, which at this writing has close to four million members. Membership to the group grew exponentially right before the election—inspiring millions to share their stories and spawning chapters at the state and local level, popular culture references, and a book to capture the spirit of the movement. In several posts at both the national and local levels, Pantsuit Nation followers discussed the social action projects started at Mio Studio. Likewise, the Pantsuit Nation method, model, and style influenced the stories that locals retold in Lancaster. Of particular interest were the ways that tellers incorporated Mio Studio jewelry into those narratives and performances.

The story behind the social action projects at Mio Studio resonated with political candidates and dignitaries over the course of the election season as well. Christina Hartman, a candidate for the US Congress in Pennsylvania's 16th District during the 2016 election, was a supporter of Mio Studio before the election and was one of the first to pick up a "Nasty Woman" charm to wear on the campaign trail. Christina also was one of the first to talk openly about the larger cultural significance of the jewelry within the Lancaster community. She felt that the jewelry had coded meanings associated with it and that she knew that someone was safe to talk to if she or he was wearing a piece of jewelry from Mio Studio. Even outside of the political action items, Erica and Mai's signature jewelry has a very recognizable sculptural quality to it. Like other supporters, Hartman posted photographs of herself wearing the "Nasty Woman" necklace.

Local political candidates themselves would stop in to pick up a piece of jewelry, or the jewelry would be gifted to them by a community member. Dale Hamby, a candidate for the Pennsylvania House of Representatives in the 100th District in Pennsylvania, would often wear his "Bad Hombre" necklace to events and was responsible for gifting Madeleine Albright a "Nasty Woman" necklace during her visit to Lancaster. Hartman posted a picture of her and Madeleine Albright at the event, and commentators noted their "Nasty Woman" necklaces.

In the weeks before the election, men and women of all ages came in to the gallery to share stories on a daily basis about why this particular election was so significant to them. There was a sense of optimism, a shared collective identity, and themes of love, hope, equality, and courage. After the election, there was a marked shift in rhetoric. Men and women of all ages still regularly came in to the gallery to share their stories but instead were now asking how they could resist, who they could turn to for comfort, and how they could organize and show support for one another. Erica and Mai started to modify the messages on their jewelry as a result to reinforce a message of resistance and to promote peace and equality. Necklaces and charms with #Resist on them began to surface immediately. Images and notes to Erica and Mai changed in tone as well. Megan writes, "While I'm still an emotional wreck about all this, today I'm thankful for artists that remind us of unity and inspire hope. Thank you. Would you be able to make these into earrings? I was thinking 'love' on one and 'all' on the other." Megan was not alone, as several customers thanked Erica for helping them heal.

Erica and Mai started to encourage customers to customize future protest pins with phrases that mattered most to them. Charms were next created that featured "Smash the Patriarchy," "Black Lives Matter," and specific spiritual and religious references. The safety pin also became a prominent postelection material culture symbol, and Erica and Mai began to incorporate the safety pin into many of their designs, providing supporters the option to place the charms on necklaces or on a safety pin. They also provided a choice in size with quarter-, dime-, and nickel-sized charms. Many customers were forthcoming with their needs and feelings. One customer posted a picture of herself wearing her new safety pin with a row of charms on it: "Love Trumps Hate," "Nasty Woman," "Pussy Grabs Back," and "Black Lives Matter." She wrote, "Is it clear where I stand? Love my new bling Erica and Mai! I am just missing #NODAPL."

In the days after the election, the grief in the gallery was palpable. Two different women came into the gallery in tears; they found comfort in being able to talk with others about their hurt and anger. On November 15, Erica responded in a more visual way. Each year downtown Lancaster has a window decorating contest. Erica publicly stated that she wanted to use the 2016 windows as "a way to move through the mourning and the grief, while adding a bit of love and peace to the streetscape." The centerpiece of the display was a hand-drawn heart with the word "peace" in multiple languages. Erica interacted with her customers and supporters throughout the process, asking for suggestions about messages to be incorporated. The display resonated with the Lancaster community and was recognized with an award during the contest.

As the studio was being decorated, an elementary-school-aged girl and her father walked in to the studio one afternoon. The little girl had heard that the gallery had "nasty woman" and other social action charms before the election. She went right away to a blue necklace with a charm on it that said "power" and asked her dad if she could put it on her Christmas list. She proceeded to tell everyone in the studio that she wanted the charm because she felt strong that week when she told others at school that she would help them if they ever needed her to stand up for them. This story, like others, confirmed that the charms provided a way for wearers to feel empowered at a time of uncertainty. The gallery was a safe space for those who needed to know that they were not alone. Rhetoric and material culture were the physical markers of that safety.

After the holidays, resistance efforts began to coalesce around the Women's Marches that were planned for January 21, 2017. One of the major postelection projects that Mio Studio initiated was a partnership between the gallery and "Seam Works," a local collective. This new collaborative effort allowed Central Pennsylvania residents to buy "pussy hats" for area marches, with all of the proceeds benefiting Planned Parenthood Keystone. While the pussy hat had larger international significance, the gallery found a way to connect the community to a popular material item of resistance—and to make it unique to Lancaster. In just over two weeks, Mio Studio was able to raise just under $5,000 for Planned Parenthood Keystone. The sale of the hats once again brought community members to the gallery to share their thoughts and experiences and plan for the upcoming marches. Many supporters customized their Mio Studio pussy hats with safety pins and charms, and they posted pictures of themselves with their new hats. Instead of sharing stories about why they were voting for Hillary Clinton, they were now sharing stories about why they were planning to participate in the Women's March. It was not uncommon to see customers wearing their hats in person at prominent City of Lancaster events, such as at a First Friday before the marches.

Mio Studio supporters wore the hats purchased at the gallery at the Women's March on Washington, the Women's March on NYC, and the Women's March on Lancaster. Like the jewelry, the hat also became part of a larger gendered performance: many supporters posted photos of themselves wearing the Mio Studio hat to document their physical presence at the marches. The Mio Studio hat also became a way to visibly identify who was from Lancaster, to reinforce solidarity within the local community, and to show public support.

The Women's March also inspired other related projects that the gallery supported and sponsored. Local activists established communication networks and promoted ways to follow through and resist. Michelle Johnson, a local photographer, created "Post-cards from the Resistance," which featured prominent images from the march. Erica also ordered a large quantity of official Women's March postcards. She offered to both address and mail either postcard for gallery visitors and also helped organize several postcard parties to generate mail for our elected representatives.

Mio Studio became known as an inclusive space to show-case other Lancaster area resistance projects. On a streetlamp pole next to the gallery, one could find notes criticizing Donald Trump and the current administration. A corner telephone pole featured a chalked message that read, "Trump Lies." Erica and Mai placed a sign out front that proclaimed, "No matter where you're from, we are glad you're our neighbor." The gallery quickly became a visible way to promote the "Welcome Your Neighbors" project; many community members stopped in to find out how to purchase their own sign. Posters would also just appear on the gallery's doorstep or taped to one of the windows. One night, a piece of poster board surfaced with two hand-drawn women on it. The sign read, "They felt the same way . . ."

The gallery also became an intersectional space. Community members came to learn how they could support the efforts of local churches, area nonprofits, the human relations commis-sion, and grassroots political campaigns. In particular, items sold at Mio Studio became a way for the LGBTQ+ community to stand together in solidarity during troubled times and periods of uncertainty. Mio Studio acted as a meeting space for the lesbian community, offering unique social opportunities such as Trans/

Queer Yoga and evening events. Mio Studio sponsored and supported area LGBTQ+ initiatives through the LGBT Center of Central PA and Lancaster Pride, and they also facilitated unique opportunities for the lesbian community to bond over a shared expressive and material culture. After the election, there was a morning meet-up to discuss ways that the community could influence local legislative efforts and be a more visible force in the community.

Postelection exhibits at Mio Studio continued to feature LGBTQ+ artists and themes and raised awareness of important issues. Local potter Dustin Horne produced rainbow-colored comma ornaments and area photographers highlighted images of former Pride-related events in Central Pennsylvania. In May of 2017, Mio Studio mounted a special exhibit to commemorate the life of Michael Headings—a member of the Lancaster LGBTQ+ community who had tragically passed away. The exhibit, entitled "Hope: Celebrating the Life and Legacy of Michael Headings," featured twenty-one pieces of art that were a part of Michael's personal collection. The exhibit marked the first time that the Headings collection was available for public exhibition. On display were original pieces of art by other local LGBTQ+ artists Freiman Stoltzfus and Victor Capecce, as well as signed prints by Steve Walker and Myles Antony. Michael was very involved with the LGBT Center of Central PA and the Common Roads youth program. One of the main goals of the exhibit was to give hope to the LGBTQ+ community, especially youth, and to reassure anyone that might be struggling with their identity that they were never alone. Mio Studio was the perfect location for the exhibit, as Michael often visited "Gallery Row" for First Friday. Michael also treasured a pair of cufflinks that Erica and Mai had made for him. The exhibit, like the community posters and jewelry on display, reinforced the role of the studio as a facilitator of critical community dialogue.

The social action projects discussed thus far demonstrate the importance of identity politics and place-based identity and question the points of intersection between lesbian and feminist identities in Lancaster. Grassroots movements, such as the ones occurring at Mio Studio, also provide an effective framework for documenting the larger folklore of resistance within the LGBTQ+ community. Elaine Lawless's 1998 article "Claiming Inversion: Lesbian Constructions of Female Identity as Claims for Authority" examines what it means to be both a female and a lesbian in Columbia, Missouri. Lawless deconstructs the lesbian aesthetic and observes how those within the lesbian community read other lesbian bodies, as well as how those outside the community read the dress, mannerisms, hairstyles, and bodies of lesbians.

Mio Studio's jewelry exemplifies what it means to be both a female and lesbian in Lancaster. The jewelry has become a part of both a local feminist and lesbian aesthetic and is a way to disrupt cultural norms in a conservative area. To be a "Nasty Woman" is to be someone who defies cultural expectations. To visibly wear the jewelry in the Lancaster community means that one's body could be read in different ways depending on whether one is within the lesbian community, outside of it, wearing it within the City of Lancaster or outside of it. What markers, if any, distinguish between feminist and lesbian identities in this case? A feminist who does not identify as lesbian or bisexual but who supports the social action projects at Mio Studio, is understood to at least be aware of the larger social and cultural impact that the project has in the Lancaster community. While "Nasty Woman" was an intersectional rallying cry, it was not a uniquely lesbian one. And yet the Mio Studio iteration of the "Nasty Woman" rhetoric was meant to be subversive in a different way—intended to queer the narrative of progressive thought in Lancaster.

Overall, the LGBTQ+ community was successful at strategically responding to conservative rhetoric throughout the 2016 election season. When Rush Limbaugh asserted that lesbian farmers were a threat to rural America, RAYGUN responded with an "America Needs Lesbian Farmers" T-shirt in John Deere's signature green and yellow colors. In a 2011 interview on Political

Vindication Radio, which was reprinted in the *New York Times*, Steve Bannon talked about the reasons that he felt progressive women were uncomfortable with conservative women such as Sarah Palin or Ann Coulter:

> That's why there are some unintended consequences of the women's liberation movement.
>
> That, in fact, the women that would lead this country would be pro-family, they would have husbands, they would love their children. They wouldn't be a bunch of dykes that came from the Seven Sisters schools up in New England. That drives the left insane and that's why they hate these women. (Bannon 2011)

Leaders at the Seven Sisters universities responded in a public statement that can be viewed on Smith College's website and in an article for *Inside Higher Ed*. Members of the LGBTQ+ community repurposed Bannon's words: Teespring produced a T-shirt that read "One of those dykes from a Seven Sisters school." All proceeds from the T-shirt sales benefited the Trevor Project. Not only those that identified as lesbians were consuming this rhetoric. As we try to define a fourth wave of feminism, and understand its complicated relationship to digital technology, we find a marked cultural shift in attitude in the twenty-first century. We have moved away from an earlier period of time in which lesbians were referred to as the "lavender menace" and did not feel at home within the larger feminist movement, to a time in which the ideal feminist for some is intersectional and identifies as queer. In 2019 is it easier for a feminist to reclaim the word "dyke" than it is to identify with Sarah Palin?

The commodification of queer identities was an integral part of the 2016 election story, just as the rhetoric and material culture of resistance was an integral part of LGBTQ+ consumer culture. Erica's identity as a prominent lesbian business owner in Lancaster reinforced the authenticity of the social action projects she initiated. While Erica and Mai were not creating the charms as a means to promote the lesbian community, neither were the charms intended for a strictly queer audience. Yet the act of consuming items produced at Mio Studio was a way of supporting a Latinx lesbian and ensuring that those voices would be heard: the charms were about more than just one's political identity.

As folklorists we often study variations on traditions and ways in which material forms can disrupt cultural norms. The American Folklore Society currently has an LGBTQIA section, but more scholarship is needed in this area to better understand how one's sex, gender, or sexual orientation impacts the transmission of ideas, affects cultural variations, and disrupts heteronormative expectations. Although feminist scholarship has appeared in the *Journal of American Folklore*, a disproportionate number of times, lesbian-feminist scholarship has been quite limited. Jeana Jorgensen, in her 2010 article "Political and Theoretical Feminisms in American Folkloristics: Definition Debates, Publication Histories, and the Folklore Feminists Communication" noted that a search of the word "feminist" in issues of the *Journal of American Folklore* yielded 161 results, and "feminism" yielded 65 results. Nine years later, "feminist" still yields only 284 results and "feminism" 100 results. By comparison, the word "lesbian" yields even fewer results at 46, and "lesbian feminism" at only 14. Jorgensen was mostly concerned with how, as folklorists, we understand feminism and how we appropriate it in our work. In 2019 I would argue that folklorists who incorporate feminist and queer theories must be both the theoretical and political feminists Jorgensen defines. One must be just as familiar with Butler, hooks, and Anzaldua as one is with Radner, Mills, Stoeltje, Turner, and Kousaleos.[3]

The Mio Studio example demonstrates how feminism can transcend its theoretical underpinnings to result in tangible political action. Folklorists should not only strive to incorporate feminism but also aim to examine, and perhaps even generate, feminist responses. Kay Turner, for example, not only examines the performative nature of feminism and looks at folklore through a queer lens; she also is a prosumer of feminist rhetoric and material culture. Margaret Mills in her 1993 article for *Western Folklore*, "Feminist Theory and the Study of Folkore: A Twenty-Year Trajectory toward Theory," concludes by saying that "the folklorist's task is to continue to reveal how communities of thought and expression (including academic ones) *are* communities of action (including political action)." As feminist folklorists, it is our responsibility to document and highlight who is moving feminist and queer theory from an academic realm into the public sphere.

While Erica and Mai are not feminist theorists in an academic sense, they still have an understanding of the historical antecedents of feminism, as well as contemporary debates and key figures. Like current feminist scholarship, Erica and Mai always wanted to reinforce that the feminist resistance Mio Studio was promoting was intersectional. It is important to note the charms that they created that featured "Black Lives Matter" and "Chinga La Migra" (which translates to "Fuck the Border Police"). For several months Erica's personal Facebook profile photo was Liza Donovan's *Hear Our Voice*. The Amplifier Foundation received over five thousand poster design submissions for the Women's March. Five images, including Donovan's, were ultimately selected and were able to be downloaded for free prior to the march. Donovan's poster featured a white, tan, and brown arm wrapped around a black one. The black arm is reaching upward and forms a torch. The poster reads, "Hear Our Voice: Women's March on Washington, January 21, 2017."

The Donovan poster was on display in the gallery's window in January and February of 2017 after the "Peace" holiday display came down. The public display of *Hear Our Voice* was a way to demonstrate to the community that Mio Studio was once again aware of national conversations that were taking place around the art of resistance. Erica and Mai encouraged others to print out and display the posters as well. Today, the Amplifier Foundation has a touring exhibition that features sixty new submissions that were never seen before. On their website the foundation categorizes itself as an "art machine for social change." A counter on the website speaks to the reach of this vernacular art form: "26 artists, 677,892 free graphics downloaded in 190 countries, 195,00 wheatpaste posters distributed, and 165,000 stickers distributed." These large numbers would not have been possible without smaller distribution networks, such as the one at Mio Studio, supporting these efforts.

There is also a spiritual aspect to the social action projects at Mio Studio. Some viewed the jewelry as a physical manifestation of feminist spirituality, the gallery as a sacred space, and the charms as lived religion. Marie Cartier, in her 2013 book, *Baby, You Are My Religion: Women, Gay Bars and Theology before Stonewall*, talks about the ways in which gay bars functioned as centers of community for the lesbian community in the way that churches sometimes do for others. A similar argument could be made about Mio Studio over the course of the election. There was a relationship between Erica and Mai and the former chaplain at Franklin & Marshall College, Rev. Susan Minasian, as well as the Unitarian Universalist Church in the Chestnut Hill neighborhood of Lancaster.

In October 2016 Rev. Susan Minasian commissioned Mio Studio to make earrings and necklaces with "Nasty Rev" forged on it for a local group of clergy members. Minasian subsequently posted photos of herself in her religious vestments and wearing both a Mio Studio pussy hat and her Nasty Rev jewelry at the Women's March. Rev. Minasian was public in her support of equality and was also one of the founders of the Lancaster Interfaith Coalition. The Lancaster newspapers interviewed Minasian about her role in the community and her efforts at coordinating the Lancaster Interfaith Coalition Vigil of Solidarity and Peace the evening before the election. Minasian also posted the following message on social media about the significance of the "Nasty Rev." rhetoric:

Let me just add this. I am a fighter in what I think is the best sense of what it means to be a fighter. I am a survivor and a thriver. I am a mother bear when it comes to the people I love and the people I am called to serve. Just because I am a pastor and just because I believe in peace and love . . . NEVER misunderstand that for not being able to protect, defend and being a warrior for justice. I will listen and I will pray. I will speak and I will read. At the end of the day . . . I am a NASTY REV. (Minasian 2016)

The ways in which Mio Studio's social action projects resonated with area religious groups is significant. Other charms featured the three jewels of Buddhism, "Buddha, Dharma, Sangha." Other customers were also concerned with peace. One woman writes the following:

Thank you Erica Millner. Gonna be a long week. . I have been socially and respectfully quiet. . this is all I will say . . . may the games of this last week begin and end with our people coming together and getting thru this difficult time. . and may God or whom ever you worship, bless us all to get this whole crazy thing worked out and may we be respectful and loving in whatever we do not agree. (Skiles 2016)

The post was also accompanied by both the praying hands emoji and the heart emoji.

It is important to understand not only who was consuming the rhetoric of resistance that Erica and Mai forged, but also why they were consuming it. For many, those reasons were not strictly about their gender identity. Instead, the reasons were multifaceted and often spoke to issues of race, class, and spirituality. Historical and rhetorical analysis of the social action projects at Mio Studio is just one component; digital ethnography as well as other ethnographic methods, including participant observation, also aided in understanding why the rhetoric resonated with customers and supporters. The attitudes and desires of those that viewed Mio Studio as a safe space before, during, and after the 2016 election were not always discernible. At times I felt that I had both an emic and etic view of the cultural exchanges that were taking place.

Then there was the physicality of the pieces themselves, the deliberate decision to work primarily with metals, and the use of a form that, in some cases, resembled military-style dog tags. Erica and Mai used craft, and already recognizable forms of adornment, to mobilize vernacular communities of resistance. Mio Studio was not alone in this effort. The 2016 election season was a platform to further highlight the many different ways that contemporary craft could be used as a form of protest. As folklorists, we should continue to be concerned with the intersection of both traditional arts and contemporary craft and the rhetoric of resistance in this current political climate. Betsy Peterson, in a 2011 article, "Folk and Traditional Arts and Social Change," in *A Working Guide to the Landscape of Arts for Change*, speaks of the reasons behind her interest in this intersection: "Folk and traditional arts allow us to use and adapt what is at hand to voice personal yet fundamental collective desires—to name and interpret our own experiences, to test our own boundaries, and to affirm cultural continuity in the face of social concerns." Likewise, Bruce Metcalf (2002) talks about craft as a "social movement" and a "vehicle in which to construct meaning"—arguing that "craft is a collective attempt to relocate personal meaning in a largely indifferent world."

We can compare current trends with how crafters have historically used their art to peacefully resist around the world. Whether it has been in the American South, in Palestine, or in Chile, the rhetoric of resistance has a long history in our field, for example, through protest songs and quilts. Christine Garlough's 2008 article in the *Journal of American Folklore* took a global perspective; she looks at the political uses of folklore in India and studying how Indian feminists used street theater to draw attention to concerns amongst women. There have also been notable exhibits in our field in this realm, such as the 1999 Philadelphia Folklore

Project exhibit, entitled *Folk Arts of Social Change*. After the 2016 election, New York's City Lore looked at protest signs as folk art for an exhibit entitled *The Art of Protest*. Occupy Wall Street, September 11, and now the Women's March have all generated folk art responses that need to be studied and documented.

After the Women's March, projects at Mio Studio continued to focus on contemporary rhetoric and adapt to current community needs. "Nevertheless, she persisted" earrings, "reclaiming my time" necklaces, and new charms that said "refugees welcome here" and "smash the patriarchy" continued to appear through July of 2019. Lists of group meetings and area events could be found at the gallery, and local groups would often have tables on the sidewalk to promote their cause on First Friday. After being at 154 North Prince Street for almost a decade, Erica and Mai made the difficult decision to permanently close Mio Studio on July 27, 2019. Rising rent costs on gallery row, the continued gentrification of Lancaster city, and Erica and Mai's desire to travel with their art, all contributed to the final decision. The local community expressed shock and sadness. Lancaster's newspaper ran a story, and the mayor's office presented a commendation to Erica and Mai for their service to the community. The final exhibit at Mio Studio was a photography exhibit entitled "Stonewall Lives: Reflecting on WorldPride." Some of the last charms that Erica and Mai made had "latinx," "pussy power," "queer," "punk," "resist," and "radical" stamped on them. Appropriately, one of the last charms sold at Mio Studio was one that had "dyke" on it. A young teenage girl who was visiting Lancaster wanted to purchase the "dyke" charm as both a memento of her trip and an outward material symbol of her identity. As we look ahead to the 2020 election, it is hard to envision a Lancaster city without Mio Studio, without a safe space for these interactions and exchanges.

The use of feminist rhetoric on material forms was not limited to Mio Studio and only continues to grow in 2019. One can easily still find commercially produced items with a click of a button—a "Nevertheless, she persisted" T-shirt, a "reclaiming my time" coffee mug, and a "smash the patriarchy" pen set. What will always make the use of the feminist rhetoric at Mio Studio unique, however, are the ways in which Erica and Mai literally forged that rhetoric by hand, used the cultural variations they created as a vehicle to inspire future storytelling and cultural exchange, and effectively disrupted cultural norms and heteronormative perspectives in a conservative region. While, on its own, the Mio Studio case study is a valuable snapshot of the folklore of resistance at the local level, it is above all meant to serve as a call to other folklorists to document the culture of resistance, especially queer feminist resistance, that is flourishing in their own communities. Trends that are happening in Lancaster city are certainly happening across the country, and around the globe, with distinct regional variations in rhetoric, form, materials, and audience. An emergent expressive culture, combined with new material cultures of resistance and innovative methods for the transmission of stories online, has allowed new vernacular feminist communities to rise and for participants to heal, feel empowered, learn from one another, and prepare for future action in this current political climate.

Notes

1. Erica and Mai moved to Lancaster in 2003 and had a workshop in downtown Lancaster prior to moving to the Prince Street location in 2010.

2. Erica and Mai's work has been featured in a number of publications, including *Lancaster Online* and *La Voz Lancaster.*

3. For important works in feminist folklore, see Polly Stewart's entry in the *Encyclopedia of American Folklife* on feminist folklorists; the 1987 special issue of the *Journal of American Folklore*; Nicole Kousaleos, 1999. "Feminist Theory and Folklore," *Folklore Forum* 30 (1–2):19–34; and works such as Dána-Ain Davis and Christa Craven, *Feminist Ethnography: Thinking through Methodologies, Challenges, and Possibilities* (2016), *Christa Craven and Dána-Ain Davis, Feminist Activist Ethnography: Counterpoints to Neoliberalism in North America* (2013), Susan Hollis, Linda Pershing, and M. Jane Young, *Feminist Theory and the Study of Folklore* (1993), | Rosan A. Jordon and Susan J. Kalcik, *Women's Folklore, Women's Culture* (1985), and Joan Radner, *Feminist Messages: Coding in Women's Folk Culture* (1993).

Works Cited

Bannon, Steve. 2011. Interview on Political Vindication Radio. Cited in *New York Times*, "Stephen Bannon and Breitbart News in Their Words," by Daniel Victor and Liam Stack, November 14, 2016. https://www.nytimes.com/2016/11/15/us/politics/stephen-bannon-breitbart-words.html.

Knapp, Tom. 2015. Found Objects as Art: Local Jewelry Designers Earn Spot at Prestigious Smithsonian Show. Lancaster Online, April 22. http://lancasteronline.com/features/found-objects-as-art-local-jewelry-designers-earn-spot-at/article_928b7816-e91a-11e4-b7c1-9720c24f675f.html.

Lawless, Elaine J. 1991. Women's Life Stories and Reciprocal Ethnography as Feminist and Emergent. *Journal of Folklore Research* 28(1):35–60.

Minasian, Susan. 2016. Facebook, November 9.

Metcalf, Bruce. 2002. Contemporary Craft: A Brief Overview. In *Exploring Contemporary Craft: History, Theory, and Critical Writing*, edited by Jean Johnson. Toronto: Coachhouse Books.

Mills, Margaret. 1993. Feminist Theory and the Study of Folkore: A Twenty-Year Trajectory toward Theory. *Western Folklore* 52(2–4):173–92.

Peterson, Betsy. 2011. Folk and Traditional Arts and Social Change. In *A Working Guide to the Landscape of Arts for Change*. Washington, DC: Americans for the Arts.

Puglise, Nicole. 2016. "Pussy Grabs Back" Becomes Rallying Cry for Female Rage against Trump." *Guardian*, October 10. https://www.theguardian.com/us-news/2016/oct/10/donald-trump-pussy-grabs-back-meme-women-twitter.

Skiles, Christine. 2016. Facebook. November 1.

Sullivan, Kathlene. 2016. Note in Mia Studio. November 17.

Wenger, Suzette. 2016. 120 People Gather in Lancaster with Message of Peace on Eve of Divisive Election. November 7. http://lancasteronline.com/news/pennsylvania/people-gather-in-lancaster-with-message-of-peace-on-eve/article_e5d61cc0-a551-11e6-9e0d-0387853444c4.html.

PAID AND PROFESSIONAL PROTESTORS?

NARRATIVES OF RESISTANCE, RHETORICS OF DISEMPOWERMENT

Adam D. Zolkover

On February 6, 2017—a bit more than two weeks after the January 21 Women's March—this exchange took place on FOX News between *Fox & Friends* host Brian Kilmeade and then White House press secretary Sean Spicer:

> "Do you sense," host Brian Kilmeade asks, "instead of being an organic disruption, do you sense that there is an organized push-back and people are being paid to protest?"
>
> "Oh, absolutely," Spicer replied. "I mean, protesting has become a profession now. They have every right to do that, don't get me wrong. But I think we need to call it what it is. It's not these organic uprisings that we have seen over the last several decades. The tea party was a very organic movement. This has become a very paid, Astroturf-type movement." (Bump 2017)

Neither section of this bifurcated answer—that protestors have been paid, and that protesting has evolved from a grassroots

expression to a professional activity—originated in the Trump era, in this political moment, or with Sean Spicer. From the podium at his presidential campaign rallies in 2016, Donald Trump made claims about paid protestors (CQ Transcriptions 2016). And claims about professional protestors exist within a dark political tradition in the United States—from segregationist politicians like Alabama governor James E. Folsom and Louisiana senator Alan J. Ellender, who called supporters of school desegregation "professional outside agitators" (*Philadelphia Inquirer* 1956; *Pittsburgh Post-Gazette* 1956) in the 1950s, to opponents of organized labor who used similar language to rebuke work stoppages as early as 1896 (*Philadelphia Inquirer*, 1896).

Yet in how they characterize the opposition, both sections of Spicer's answer mark trends among Republican politicians and right-leaning media outlets that go beyond dismissing protestors' grievances. The claims perpetrate a kind of role reversal that casts those in power as helpless victims of a faceless conspiracy, fueled by dark money, in retribution for their efforts to clean up corruption—to drain the swamp, so to speak. And in doing so, the claims collapse the complex and variable motivations of protestors into a single, digestible narrative that conveys the feel of truth, in no small part because it meets the cognitive and moral expectations of its audience.

Pamela Adams of the conservative *Constitution Blog* exemplifies both this twinned narrative and its power by locating the source of protestors' pay, and a conspiracy to foil the new administration, on ground that would be familiar to many of the most extreme elements of the conservative movement. Just days after the Women's March, she wrote that Hungarian-American investor, philanthropist, and activist "George Soros funded over 50 organizations partnering and participating in the March for Women's Rights. Part of that funding went straight into the protestors' pockets. They weren't there for rights," she said. "They were there for riches" (2017).

The force of the claim derives in no small part from Adams's employment of a set of vernacular rhetorical techniques that resemble those used in the discourse of legend. In his 2008 article "Legendry and the Rhetoric of Truth," Elliott Oring writes that "statements that are accepted as obviously true" bear little comment, but legends, which "make what are perceived to be extraordinary claims . . . require the deployment of a rhetoric to allay doubts and foil challenges" (Oring 2008: 129). He offers a catalogue of tropes calibrated to accomplish this, which he presents "in terms of Aristotle's categories of *ethos*, *logos*, and *pathos*" (130). In this case Adams's appeals to "witnesses and experts" and to the preexisting beliefs of her audience are particularly relevant (130). In terms of the former, Adams invokes the research of "renowned author Asra Q Nomani"—a freelance journalist who, in a tweet, suggested that stories like these mischaracterize her work (Adams 2017; Nomani 2017). And in terms of the latter, Adams chooses a comfortable villain in George Soros, who was a frequent object of conservative ire throughout the Obama administration. Almost as relevant in this case is Oring's explanation of "story logic" or our willingness to "suspend our disbelief when we encounter premises or behaviors that are out of keeping with how the real world works" (Oring 2008:149). On its face the notion of paying protestors makes little practical sense. But in terms of dramatic effect, it is highly persuasive.

Extreme conservative media, throughout 2017, replicated this formula in their discussion of protests. *Breitbart* contributor James Delingpole wrote that the Women's March is "basically just another tentacle of George Soros—the sinister, cat-stroking destroyer-of-worlds who . . . funded no fewer than 56 of the partners involved in the march" (2017). In the far-right *NewsBusters*, author Aly Nielsen wrote that "more than a quarter of" groups who participated in the Women's March "have been funded by liberal billionaire George Soros" (2017). And in a later article for *NewsBusters*, author Corrine Weaver called the event the "Soros-funded Women's March" (2017).

Even after the 2016 election, it is tempting to label reporting from organizations like *Breitbart* and *NewsBusters* as marginal—the overinflated writing of professional provocateurs. But these articles seem to both capture and contribute to a widely held narrative. A week after the 2017 Women's March, the *Washington Times* reported on a Public Policy Polling survey finding that 38 percent of Trump voters believed that George Soros had paid protestors to attend, and another 29 percent of Trump voters were unsure (Blake 2017; Public Policy Polling 2017). And reader comments from *Breitbart* illustrate how this fits into an existing ideological frame. In response to its report about Soros's funding of "more than 50 'partners' of anti-Trump women's march," a subset of commenters identify Soros as an existential threat to the United States: "Soros definitely needs to be kicked out of America. He's responsible for our fellow citizens being harmed and even killed, he's a threat to American citizens and the country!" (Klein 2017). Another comment type plays up the narrative of Soros as a sinister man in the shadows: "[Angela] Merkel is just a Soros Puppet like Obama & Hillary. Globalist/Open Borders-NWO, Soros is just Front Man for the Bilderberg Group" (Klein 2017). Still others refer to him "demonic," suggest that he was a Nazi collaborator or a communist, and call for him to be deported to Russia, where there is supposedly a warrant out for his arrest (Klein 2017).

The Glenn Beck–associated website *TheBlaze* had no need to use George Soros's name to elicit similar conspiratorial claims among its readers. Commenters on two articles about the People's March for Science, neither of which mentions Soros, repeatedly cite him as the march's funder (Haskins 2017; Lee 2017). They claim that protest signs are printed using George Soros's money and describe attendees as pro-Soros internet trolls disguised as scientists. These comments underline the narrative that resistance to Donald Trump's election cannot have grown organically—that protestors' actions are informed by one primary, external motivator that itself is marred by ill intent. And they underline a kind of diabolical story logic—that there is one prime mover of all these events.

In the direct aftermath of the 2017 Women's March, conservative politicians were less eager to name a single puppet master. This may be especially true in the case of George Soros, whose Jewish heritage lends the narrative an unsavory anti-Semitic quality. Yet the basic frame—of professional protestors and outside agitators masquerading as angry constituents—was apparent in the mainstream of Republican national politics. Throughout February and March of 2017, Republican legislators—including Steve King of Iowa, Jason Chaffetz of Utah, Cory Gardner of Colorado, and Pat Toomey of Pennsylvania—claimed that town hall attendees had been paid to protest and ask irate questions. They also insisted that constituents telephoning their offices were paid agitators from out of state (Alexandersen 2017; Clark 2017; Hayworth 2017; Rupar 2017). Their statements would seem to dismiss the possibility that concerned citizens could be motivated en masse to express anger at the agenda of a party that had just won across the board at the polls. And as with more explicit Soros narratives, they would seem to suggest that citizens motivated by activist organizations and interest groups are by definition contractors, discredited by virtue of the fact that they are engaged in a project not their own.

Claims of paid and professional protestors, and all that they imply, underline the problem of collapsing the variable motivations of individuals who see themselves as Trump resisters into a single narrative. The intent of Trump administration operatives like Spicer—or Republican politicians like King, Chaffetz, Gardner, and Toomey—may well be to discredit only particular modes of political action. But the *effect* is to disempower and dehumanize. Those narratives transform individual protestors into characters in a drama who are twice mediated: first through the narrative frame of George Soros, or whoever purportedly pulls their strings; and second through the animating hand of conspiracists who have rewritten protestors as akin to fiction. Within this doubled frame, protestors cannot determine and weigh their own motivations, they risk nothing by their presence in public, and they cannot form the kinds of grassroots organizations that might become the basis for political action. The level of disrespect that this implies is well illustrated by one informant's incredulous and adamant response when I brought the narrative up in an interview. "No," she told me. "I was not paid by George Soros. I was not paid by anybody. . . . This was a fully self-funded enterprise."

As part of this project, I conducted extended interviews with two women—sisters—who have become more politically active since the 2016 election. One of the women, a retail professional, attended both the 2017 Women's March and the March for Science in Philadelphia. The other, a scientist and museum professional, attended only the March for Science. Taken together, their stories offer a more useful counternarrative to these claims than an analysis that, in elucidating the problematic qualities of narratives about paid and professional protestors, further abstracts individuals on the ground. They offer a window into the motivations that underlie these protests, and the risks and benefits of participation, which stands in stark contrast to the singularity of the narrative above.

Asked to explain how she became involved in protests against the Trump administration, the museum professional explained that her motivation was both personal and professional:

> As a genotypic person of color—I may not be phenotypically of color, but I am definitely genotypically a person of color, and I have many family members who are physically people of color, and I was legitimately scared for them. So I had this huge amount of anxiety for them. . . . I have family that won't come to visit because it's too risky. I have family I haven't seen in a long time because they used to travel here quite frequently, and now they . . . don't.

The situation in 2017 was no less a source of concern in her professional life:

I am deeply entrenched in grant-writing, and we have grants out to the NEH, NSF, Fulbright, IMLS, and they can't give us assurances in many cases of what the funding situation will be like. One of the things we're trying to assess is the cost-benefit analysis of putting a significant amount of time into a grant where your grant could be severely reduced in terms of money if you even get it, because they reduced the amount where institutions were applicable. . . . I like to know . . . what my chances are, is there going to be funding for next year, how much, what's the disbursement. . . . And even our federal budget is day-to-day practically. And so, that again, is another layer of anxiety.

The retail professional answered the same question by focusing less on her social positioning than on the political landscape writ broadly: in the past, she often disagreed with presidents' policies, but she never thought that the president was malicious. Donald Trump, she told me, is malicious.

The two women noted several other reasons for their protest activity, including climate change, reproductive rights, and the undermining of science as a mode of systematic inquiry. The retail professional also called it an issue of respect. Her resistance to Donald Trump as a political figure began early in his campaign. "The more he opened his mouth, when he mocked a disabled reporter, the way he spoke about Megyn Kelly—she must be bleeding out of her 'I-don't-know-what'—so many things." The Women's March especially, she said, was a direct response to people's perception of Donald Trump's misogyny and the statements and policies that have followed it.

Both women also reported that part of the power of protesting, from their perspective, derived from speaking out in the face of risk. The museum professional brought her kindergarten-aged son to the March for Science and reported that she "had an exit strategy if it was going to be dangerous." "My mother was there," she said, "and she was going to take him right back home on the train." Crowds constitute a significant source of stress for her, which kept her from participating in the Women's March. "I couldn't go to that because I was really scared of the crowds, and I was more anxious," she told me. And yet, "when the Science March came along, I basically said 'suck it up, you're doing this.' And I did." But "anytime you go into a situation like that," she said, "you're taking personal and professional risks." In this sense, she was not alone:

> I know a lot of people [at the March for Science] who work for large scientific corporations or maybe they work for a large institute that didn't officially sanction it—you are taking a personal risk. Everything's out there. You could find your name out there in the paper with your picture, and a lot of employers don't like that. So, there's definitely risks in being labeled as pro-science, pro-evolution, pro-education. And we're noticing that more and more in this day and age. Where you really have to live your life as if everything is going to be permanently recorded.

For both of these women and for their colleagues, the choice to increase their level of political activity and political visibility speaks to the point of protesting: it is an act of defiance in the face of political power. Presence, in the context of public assembly, implies precarity—a vulnerability channeled both through the inevitability of being seen and through the possibility of being acted upon as a result of that presence. But as Judith Butler comments in *Notes toward a Performative Theory of Assembly*, presence is also a political message, and "taking up space and obdurately living, is already an expressive action." As Butler writes, "the bodies assembled 'say' we are not disposable, even if they stand silently" (2017:17).

One of the features of the narrative of paid and professional protestors is that it attempts to obfuscate both the stated and unstated messages of the protests. James Delingpole at *Breitbart* writes—in a mode that wavers between snarky and willfully dense—that the purpose of the Women's March was inscrutable.

"Has anyone actually worked out yet what that Women's March over the weekend was all about?" he asks. And he offers that perhaps marchers were angry over "a forgotten anniversary, . . . an unnoticed new hair do [*sic*], [or a] . . . toilet seat left up" (Delingpole 2017).

TheBlaze suggests that participants in the March for Science were deceptive about their purpose—according to *TheBlaze*, marchers may have claimed it was a defense of science, but their real goal was a defense of government funding and the maintenance of a political system that rewards scientific activities friendly to a preexisting (liberal) ideology. Its leaders, one article suggests, are "climate alarmists who have been vocal opponents of Trump's decision to scale back climate-change-related funds." The article concludes with a question to readers: "Is the March of Science really about protecting science, or is it motivated by a desire to protect the tens of billions of taxpayer dollars the science-research industry has received over the past decade and promoting the theory humans are destroying the planet by causing global warming?" (Haskins 2017).

Moreover, redefining protestors as freelancers seems calibrated to undermine the political impact of presence. Claims by proponents of these theories leave room to acknowledge the reality that yes, hundreds of thousands of people made themselves visible in dozens of cities during the two events. But those protestors' presence does not constitute the kind of vulnerability we might assume and, by extension, does not convey any kind of genuine political message, because many of those bodies were there under contract. They are not really aggrieved. They are, to borrow a term from conspiracies about the February 14, 2,018 shooting at Marjory Stoneman Douglas High School in Parkland, Florida, crisis actors.

Yet my informants suggest that the purpose of these protests is not obscure. Of the Women's March, the retail professional told me, "ideally, you want to have Planned Parenthood fully funded, other things—equal pay. [But also,] it's really successful at keeping people motivated and getting the right people together and connected to try to get things done." The protests are a success if "people were like 'all right, the Women's March was great. Why don't we march about this [other thing], too?'" The retail professional also said that the meaning of the March is in its visibility. "If it's acknowledged, if whatever ideas they're trying to get across, they get them across," that counts as a success.

This is where efforts to delegitimize the protests—and the protestors—are most damaging. For 38% of Trump voters to support the claim that participants in the Women's March were paid by George Soros—as the Public Policy Polling survey asserts—suggests negation not acknowledgement. By contrast, only 1 percent of Hillary Clinton voters supported the claim (2017). This suggests a widening gulf between America's two major political parties—a transformation of ideological difference into tribal affiliation that is exacerbated by, and exacerbates, the dehumanization implicit in the Soros narrative.

The 2017 Women's March and its successors did broadcast their point. Protests were covered in wide-reaching news outlets like the *New York Times*, *Washington Post*, and *San Francisco Chronicle*, as well as regional and local outlets across the country. Social media were inundated. On Twitter, Hillary Clinton thanked protestors "for standing, speaking & marching for our values," and, invoking her campaign slogan "stronger together," she called the march an invaluable display of solidarity. In her campaign memoir, *What Happened*, Clinton devotes a section to the power of the Women's March, and to acknowledging the meaningful contributions of the protestors.

However, that coverage was not equally distributed across ideological perspectives. As Kristine Nicolini and Sarah Hansen write in the *Public Relations Review*, "FOX News coverage" emphasized "specific celebrity quotes and behaviors taken out of a broader march context" and highlighted "'off message' details that did not represent the organizational strategic messaging" (2018:5). It eschewed "participant and organizer quotes within the coverage" (5). As Sean Spicer's February 6 interview with *Fox*

& *Friends* illustrates, it alluded to and even endorsed the kinds of nonfactual coverage that more extreme conservative media organizations emphasized.

Regarding claims about George Soros, the retail professional told me that "the people who believe that are not going to be swayed, anyway." But the collapse of a multitude of protestor perspectives into a singular narrative guided by a dehumanizing story logic has had significant impact on how progressive voices are heard across the board. Since the 2017 Women's March, public officials have become less shy about embracing the extreme conservative line. In October of 2018, President Trump gave it credence by tweeting that protestors of Brett Kavanaugh's nomination to the Supreme Court were "paid for by Soros and others" (Trump 2018). Senator Chuck Grassley, chair of the Senate Judiciary Committee, echoed the sentiment in a FOX Business Network interview (Chokshi 2018). And these claims came in the context of a concrete political victory for Trump and his associates over significant grassroots opposition. And so, in terms of the question of whether large-scale protests like the Women's March or the March for Science have been successful despite the noise created by conspiracist claims, the answer seems to be: not yet.

But short-term political and policy gain may not be the right measure. When I asked the retail professional about her favorite moment at the 2017 Philadelphia Women's March, she responded, "A guy put his little girl on his shoulders, and she holds up a sign and she starts a chant that's 'show me what democracy looks like,' and everybody answers 'this is what democracy looks like.' When the little girl is leading that chant, it's pretty awesome." Embedded in this kind of affirmative experience, we can glimpse an alternative frame. An atmosphere of joyful, positive comradery in the face of a hostile political climate generates its own messaging that is directed internally—toward protestors—as much as toward the world at large. In it is an emergent narrative of political action as something within the grasp of ordinary citizens with busy lives, and of a common humanity that transcends one particular political adversary.

Of course, none of this undoes the dehumanizing force or the political divisions that the narratives of paid and professional protestors create. For friends and families on opposite sides of that divide, it does not mend fences. But bleak as that sounds, the power of shared experience may vindicate the risks taken by individuals choosing to make themselves present and visible—especially if that shared experience has the potential to translate into an organized community of action that extends beyond a single march.

Works Cited

Adams, Pamela. 2017. EXPOSED: George Soros Funded Over 50 'March for Women's Rights' Partner Groups. *The Constitution Blog*. January 24. https://constitution.com/exposed-george-soros-funded-50-march-womens-rights-partner-groups/.

Alexandersen, Christian. 2017. Toomey Blames Excessive Office Calls, Emails on "People Outside of Our State" ahead of DeVos Vote. *PennLive*. February 6. http://www.pennlive.com/nation-world/2017/02/toomey_blames_excessive_office.html

Blake, Andrew. 2017. George Soros Paid Women's March Protestors, Say 1 in 3 Trump Voters: Poll. *Washington Times*, January 27. https://www.washingtontimes.com/news/2017/jan/27/george-soros-paid-womens-march-protestors-say-1-in/.

Bump, Philip. 2017. The White House and Fox Join Forces to Undermine Anti-Trump Protests as Violent and Fake. *Washington Post*, February 6. https://www.washingtonpost.com/news/politics/wp/2017/02/06/the-white-house-and-fox-join-forces-to-undermine-anti-trump-protests-as-violent-and-fake/.

Butler, Judith. 2017. *Notes toward a Performative Theory of Assembly*. Cambridge: Harvard University Press.

Chokshi, Niraj. 2018. Trump Derides Kavanaugh Protestors and Claims They Were Paid. *New York Times*, October 6. https://www.nytimes.com/2018/10/05/us/politics/trump-kavanaugh-protestors-paid.html.

Clark, Kyle. 2017. Senator Cory Gardner Reaffirms Stance That Paid Protestors Are Eclipsing Coloradans. 9news.com. February 1. http://www.9news.com/news/local/next/senator-cory-gardner-reaffirms-stance-that-paid-protestors-are-eclipsing-coloradans/395605064.

Clinton, Hillary. 2017. *What Happened*. London: Simon & Schuster.

Clinton, Hillary (@HillaryClinton). 2017. Thanks for standing, speaking & marching for our values @womensmarch. Important as ever. I truly believe we're always Stronger Together. Twitter, January 21, 2017. https://twitter.com/HillaryClinton/status/822822900239581184.

CQ Transcriptions. 2016. Donald Trump, Republican Presidential Candidate, Delivers Remarks at a Campaign Event. October 31.

Delingpole, James. 2017. Delingpole: Women's March—See What a Massive, Hillary-Shaped Bullet America Just Dodged? *Breitbart*. January 23. https://www.breitbart.com/big-government/2017/01/23/womens-march -now-do-you-see-what-a-massive-hillary-shaped-bullet-america -just-dodged/.

Haskins, Justin. 2017. Scientists Rally across US to "Defend" Science—but Closer Look Reveals a Different Motive. *TheBlaze*. April 22, 2017. https://www.the blaze.com/news/2017/04/22/scientists-rally-across-us-to-defend-science -but-closer-look-reveals-a-different-motive.

Hayworth, Bret. 2017. Steve King Alleges Paid Protestors Are Disrupting Town Halls. *Sioux City Journal*. http://siouxcityjournal.com/news/local/steve-king -alleges-paid-protestors-are-disrupting-town-halls/article_94d18c8b-848e -56a7-b1e3-edcd97d2d26d.html.

Klein, Aaron. 2017. Soros-Funded Groups Back Anti-Trump Women's March. *Breitbart*. January 12. https://www.breitbart.com/big-government/2017/01/12 /anti-trump-womens-march-backed-soros-funded-groups/.

Lee, Sarah. 2017. Just When You Thought the Marches Were Over, Here Comes the March for Science. *TheBlaze*. January 26. https://www.theblaze.com/news /2017/01/26/just-when-you-thought-the-marches-were-over-here-comes-the -march-for-science.

Nielsen, Aly. 2017. Soros Gave Nearly $90 Million to Liberal "Women's March" Partners. *NewsBusters*. January 10. https://www.newsbusters.org/blogs/busi ness/alatheia-nielsen/2017/01/10/soros-gave-nearly-90-million-liberal -womens-march.

Nicolini, Kristine M., and Sara Steffes Hansen. 2018. Framing the Women's March on Washington: Media Coverage and Organizational Messaging Alignment. *Public Relations Review* 44(1):1–10.

Nomani, Asra Q. (@AsraNomani). 2017. I dont allege "Soros paid protestors"? I say: Soros funds many march "partners." I wud like @womensmarch to reveal its funders @VerocaiCohen. Twitter, January 21. https://twitter.com /AsraNomani/status/822979952454889472.

Oring, Elliott. 2008. Legendry and the Rhetoric of Truth. *Journal of American Folklore* 121(480):127–66.

Philadelphia Inquirer. 1956. Ellender Warns against Violence. Morning edition. March 18.

Philadelphia Inquirer. 1896. The Proposed Tie-Up Proved a Failure: President Mahon Announced It Illegal and Requested Men to Return to Work. Morning Edition. January 4.

Pittsburgh Post-Gazette. 1956. Alabama U. to Appeal on Integration. February 14.

Public Policy Polling. 2017. Americans Think Trump Will Be Worst President since Nixon. January 26. http://www.publicpolicypo.lling.com/wp-content /uploads/2017/09/PPP_Release_National_12617.pdf.

Richardson, Valerie. 2017. George Soros Gave $36M to Groups behind People's Climate March. *Washington Times*, April 28. https://www.washingtontimes .com/news/2017/apr/28/george-soros-gave-36m-groups-behind-peoples -climat/.

Rupar, Aaron. 2017. Chaffetz Says Paid Protestors Are Hounding Him. Reporters Can't Find a Single One. *Think Progress* (blog). February 11. https://think progress.org/chaffetz-paid-protestors-town-hall-9f97e1f16d62/.

Trump, Donald J. 2018. The Very Rude Elevator Screamers Are Paid Professionals Only Looking to Make Senators Look Bad. Don't Fall for It! Also, Look at All of the Professionally Made Identical Signs. Paid for by Soros and Others. These Are Not Signs Made in the Basement from Love! #Troublemakers. Tweet. *@realDonaldTrump* (blog). October 5. https://twitter.com/real DonaldTrump/status/1048196883464818688?s=19.

Weaver, Corinne. 2017. Soros-Funded Women's March Organize Unhinged Protest against NRA. *NewsBusters*. July 7. https://www.newsbusters.org /blogs/culture/corinne-weaver/2017/07/07/soros-funded-womens-march -organize-unhinged-protest-against.

I CAN'T BELIEVE I STILL HAVE TO PROTEST THIS SHIT

GENERATIONAL VARIATION AND SOLIDARITY AMONG WOMEN'S MARCH PARTICIPANTS

Patricia Sawin

As a child of the 1960s and a high-school-aged participant in marches against the Vietnam War, I internalized a sense that political protest was a young person's game. Participating in the January 2017 Women's March, however, corrected that long-held misapprehension. Engaging in that protest, studying photographs shared on social media and in the press, and talking with friends and colleagues afterward convinced me not only that each generation has a distinctive role to play in the pressing social justice work of our time but also that displaying those roles to one another—as we did at the Women's March—can bridge generational divides and foster the respect essential to productive cooperation.

When I was a teenager, it seemed to me that going bodily into the streets to chant slogans and carry signs was the province of those not yet burdened with family responsibilities or invested in the status quo, those who were not old enough to vote[1] or did

not have money to contribute to political campaigns, those who would bear the brunt of the war their elders had chosen to prosecute but who did not have other ways to influence politicians' decision making. My perception of a generational division of political labor was, of course, not actually true of civil rights and Vietnam era protestors, has never been true of labor organizers, and is not true today. One might observe that those willing to put themselves in the way of grievous bodily harm to oppose injustice—from Freedom Riders who challenged the segregation of interstate buses in the 1960s to contemporary antifascist activists prepared to respond with force to white supremacist violence—often tend to be young and able bodied. Yet I know from personal experience that many of the stalwarts of North Carolina's recent Moral Monday protests against our conservative legislature are retired people older than myself, including North Carolina's band of the apron-clad Raging Grannies, who redefine older women's role from cookie baking to leading protest songs. And disabled people have been among the most visible and determined protestors against recent Republican efforts to cut Medicaid benefits; by using their mobility devices to clog the hallways of the US Capitol, they have been able to capitalize on law enforcement's reluctance to physically remove their apparently frail bodies—and the damning optics when they do.

My longstanding conviction that I could appropriately avoid participating in political protest thus speaks more to my own white privilege, overdeveloped sense of propriety, and complacency—if not downright irresponsibility or cowardice—than to any accurate analysis.[2] Despite my dissatisfaction with and explicit critique of much government policy and conduct—regarding immigration, the social safety net, defense, and women's and LGBTQ rights, at a minimum—under Democratic as well as Republican administrations, I had never stopped to ask the question "How does egalitarian reform ever happen in the United States?" (Piven 2006:21) or to learn from the evidence of times I had lived through. Theorists of social protest movements argue that "the rare intervals of nonincremental democratic reform [that works to the benefit of those without economic or coercive power] are [almost exclusively] responses to the rise of disruptive protest movements" (Piven 2006:18). Effective protest and attendant progressive change are rare, however, precisely because most people continue to believe that "if most citizens are entitled to vote in periodic elections for the persons who will hold state office, . . . government officials will be bound to take citizen preferences into account in their crucial, life-shaping decisions" (2006:2), despite abundant evidence to the contrary. As a corollary, many people, myself included, are inclined to regard disruptive activity outside the electoral process as ineffectual and even embarrassing (see Piven 2014). It was, indeed, only a couple of years before the Women's March that I felt threatened enough by my state legislature's gerrymandering, cuts to public school funding, attacks on LGBTQ rights, and meddling in higher education to begin participating in local protests after a decades-long hiatus. There have long been "numerous obstacles to the realization of [the democratic] ideal" in the United States (Piven 2006:2)—including voter disenfranchisement, gerrymandering, the need of political parties to paper over internal dissent in order to maintain a voting majority, and the translation of economic power into political power (2006:2–20). But whether relatively complacent liberals like myself were theorizing their participation in the march or simply reacting, the shocking election of Donald Trump made many of us feel that the electoral system was insufficient or broken, and the Women's March presented an immediate opportunity to take to the streets and express our critique.

Quite a few of those who participated in the Women's March on January 21, 2017, were—as signs and speeches indicated—already engaged in ongoing political and protest efforts. Still, the very numbers—an estimated 1.3 percent of the US population[3]—suggest that many marchers were like me, jolted into a need to act in a new way by their fear not only that the new administration would roll back progressive legal accomplishments but even that the election of Trump represented an existential threat to American democracy. My lingering sense that it was unusual for older people to be active protestors made me even more exhilarated by the evident participation in the march of women and allies across the age spectrum. I was thus acutely aware of the march as a show of intergenerational solidarity, an insistence that it was by no means just the young who objected to the sexism, racism, ageism, ableism, homophobia, and xenophobia; the lack of intelligence, good judgment, and simple humanity; and the appalling policy proposals of the man who had just been inaugurated president.

But while four and half million protestors on seven continents (Pressman and Chenoweth 2017) were all in the march together, people of various ages and life stages did not play precisely the same role. Members of four approximate generational cohorts—little children, maidens, mothers, and crones—were out in force. Each played a recognizable role, contributing a distinctive symbolic component to the march's overall message and effect. We shared a motivation, but each cohort had its own part to play in claiming space, refuting slurs, standing up for the range of values threatened by the Trump administration, and asserting the right of women to be ourselves, to be valued and respected at every age. Marching together enhanced the ebullient feeling of connection, strength, and possibility and helped feminists of different "waves" to appreciate one another's philosophies and contributions.

My analysis focuses on the messages that marchers with their signs and costumes communicated to one another and, via journalists' reports and copious social media sharing, to a wider audience and posterity. In Raleigh, North Carolina, where I marched, as at the mother Women's March in Washington, DC, as well as those in most other cities, including Chicago, Denver, and San Francisco, the protest attracted so many times more marchers than the organizers had anticipated that relatively few participants could actually hear the official speeches and musical performances. Participants' experience was thus primarily one of

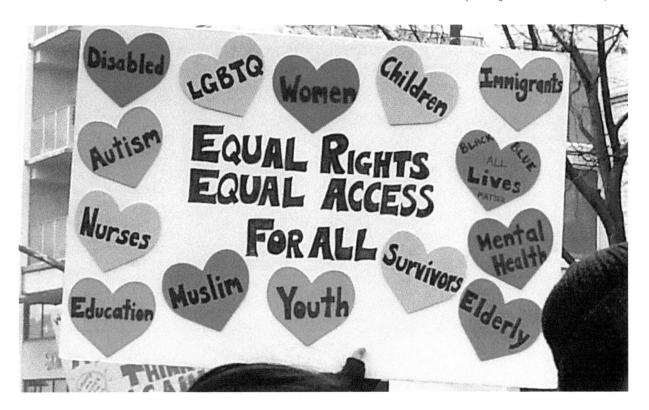

Sign naming fourteen causes the protester supports. "Equal rights, equal access for all." Raleigh, North Carolina. Photo by Patricia Sawin.

viewing and taking photographs of others' signs, hats, and costumes as we waited or moved slowly together through the streets. I realized the importance of march participants' representing to one another only in the process of doing so.

While the organizers' perspective and intentions and the inspiring remarks of the line-up of prominent feminists and celebrities—featured in other publications, including the Women's March Organizers' own *Together We Rise: The Women's March: Behind the Scenes at the Protest Heard around the World* (2018)— are also significant, I take the ground-level, marcher's view. I speak from my own experience as a determined participant who (like many) did not know quite what to expect and as both an older woman and a mother whose position made me especially sensitive to the varying roles of the generational cohorts. While I

Baby in a pussy hat being carried by her mother, Denver. Photo by Karen Deal Robinson.

have studied hundreds of photographs from marches around the world, my perspective is most thoroughly informed by my own experience in Raleigh and by sets of photographs shared with me by my colleague Leedom Lefferts, with whom I marched in Raleigh; by Karen Deal Robinson, who marched with her daughter in Denver, Colorado; and Maxine Vande Vaarst, who marched in Washington, DC. I circulated a Google survey through friend channels and received eighteen verbal testimonials from those who marched in cities and towns across the United States as well as several illuminating comments from folklorists who had heard an earlier version of this essay, which I presented at the 2017 American Folklore Society meeting.[4] I draw on these accounts and reflections to talk about marchers' motivations. I thus offer an impression, consistent with broader accounts in emphasizing the

Supergirl, Raleigh, North Carolina.

Photo by Patricia Sawin.

importance of multigenerational participation but stressing the generational distinctiveness that stood out for me.

As is the wont of festive and contestative public displays, the march was inherently and gloriously multivocalic (Bakhtin 1981). Each enactment was directed simultaneously to at least two or three different audiences. The things we did, the things we wore, and the things we said (with signs and in stories) were all, at the same time, both a vehement rejection of Trump's words and actions—often a critical parody or a directive to desist from one of his objectionable behaviors—and a confident, joyful assertion to one another of the humane, feminist values we share. We also cajoled one another not to lose hope. In response to my question "What motivated you to join the march?" some respondents stated "fear" or "anti-woman rhetoric," but others elaborated on the connection between their concern (even despair) and the power of collective, bodily presence. From Eugene, Oregon: "So disgusted and frustrated and shocked by Trump being elected despite his treatment of women and racist platform; worried about women's health care and rights; worried about immigrants and refugees and wanting to express solidarity and resistance through a huge visible platform." From Durham, North Carolina: "Disgust with the world. The need to do something, the need to move, unable to sit still. The hope of being surrounded by likeminded people. Hoping that something momentous and historic might come of this." From Los Angeles: "Feeling helpless and bereft and angry about

"Save my future." Raleigh, North Carolina. Photo by Leedom Lefferts

"We can be the change." Raleigh,
North Carolina. Photo by Leedom
Lefferts.

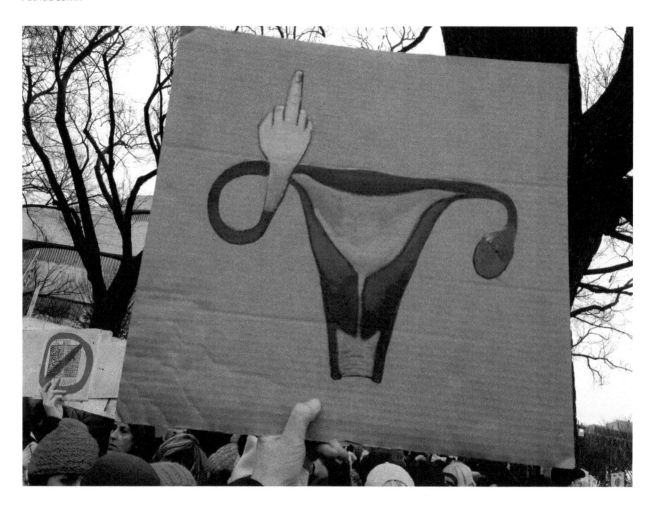

Uterus and Fallopian tubes giving the finger, Washington, DC. Photo by Maxine Vande Vaarst.

the election results, and wanting to demonstrate cohesion in constructive opposition to the politics and policies of the incoming administration." From Park City, Utah: "I often feel isolated, hopeless and fearful of the future of this country that raised me; however, when I stand shoulder-to-shoulder with my neighbors during a march I realize that America really is a remarkable place, and there are many of us who absolutely refuse to let racism, sexism, and homophobia define who we are as individuals and collectively as a society." From Berkeley, California:

A lot. But I think it more or less boils down to A. Wanting to experience the feeling that I wasn't alone in finding the course of the nation unacceptable; B. Wanting to signal to the larger world and the communities of racial minorities, women, people with disabilities, immigrants, and the LGBT that we were there to fight and that American values hadn't fundamentally changed despite this disastrous election; C. Modeling decency for my kid; D. Profound and inexpressible rage needing to find joy.

A notable feature of the Women's March, particularly in contrast to the 2016 Democratic and Republican national political conventions, then relatively fresh in people's minds, was the preponderance and variety of homemade signs. Some were very artful, while others were rough and evidently created just to get the marcher's message out on cardstock. The signs did not necessarily express original thoughts in unique form. My unscientific impression is that "Women's Rights Are Human Rights," "Girls just want to have FUNdamental rights," and "Respect my existence or expect my resistance" (in English and in Spanish) appeared more often than any others. Indeed, the simultaneous expression on any one sign of environmental, immigrant rights, antiracist, pro-science, LGBTQ, minimum wage, and reproductive rights slogans, among many others and in addition to criticisms and parodies of Trump, was a crucial part of the point. And the prevalence of social media communication before and about the march meant that many people found the message they wanted to express offered by someone who had shared a beautifully designed and printable version.

Preprinted professional signs from organizations like Planned Parenthood contributed to the overall message that we believed in all these values and opposed the new president's intentions to attack and undermine them. They also served as a reminder that we were powerful not simply as the temporary if exhilarating collective gathered that day but as members of long-standing organizations with established and practical political programs.

Camille Sleight-Price found the sign that she has carried at several marches and has also displayed in her yard, "Hate has no home here," circulated for printing on the Pantsuit Nation Facebook group. Several people I know invited their friends to come together in the days before the march to brainstorm ideas and create signs. Too busy at the beginning of a semester to attend a sign-making party, I searched the internet for meaningful quotations to reproduce. But it mattered that in so many cases individuals had at least taken the time to select and draw out a slogan that spoke to their most powerful concerns if not to create an absolutely original representation or formulation. Still, seeing marchers of various ages carrying signs with similar messages provided a background consistency against which the variation among those whose behavior emphasized generational cohort roles—child, maiden, mother, crone—stood out for me.

The presence of small children—walking, in strollers, strapped to parents' chests, riding on parents' shoulders—elicited many smiles. Babies in pussy hats and kitty costumes asserted their right to innocence now and to respect when they grow up. Little girls dressed as Superwoman encouraged us to take hope from "girl power." A grade schooler in Raleigh carried a sign that exhorted starkly, "Save my future." A woman who drove to the DC march from Michigan reported, "My six-year-old daughter did not make the drive with us, but asked me to carry a picture she drew about love so that she could be there with me in spirit." Slightly older girls inspired us with a vision of the future they could already glimpse and commit themselves to; a ten- or twelve-year-old in Raleigh held a handmade sign saying "We can be the change." Many photos on social media showed grade-school-aged children with signs that urged "No bullying"—not so subtly chastising the president for his frequent and childish attacks on the vulnerable. A toddler rode in his stroller through the Raleigh march proudly brandishing a sheet of paper covered with his scribbles; similar scenes were reported from Charlotte and other marches, sometimes with the hashtag #WokeBaby

(Wanshel 2017). Whether you took those scribbles as a representation of inchoate rage, as a determined attempt by the not-yet-literate to get a message across, or simply as practice creating signs for future demonstrations, the nonverbal message spoke volumes.

I had wondered whether parents would bring their young children, given the violence perpetrated against some anti-Trump protesters at the inauguration the day before, and the march organizers' warnings that participants should expect long days, long walks, and long lines for the port-a-potties. But those welcome little ones provided both motivation and perspective. Theirs is indeed the future we are fighting for. They will grow up fast, into a dystopian reality if we don't stop it, but we have to be dedicated to the effort for the long term. Their presence was an important part of creating a loving and lovely place in that moment and of claiming public space as a safe space for women, for children, for everyone.

Acknowledging the traditional tripartite vision of women's power, we might call the next group "maidens," although only if within "maiden" we include persons of all genders and sexualities, and if we envision the maiden as Diana the huntress stalking her prey with fierce determination. Marchers in their late teens, twenties, and thirties were by no means the only ones horrified to hear the candidate and now-president brag about the sexist objectification of their bodies. These younger adult marchers, however, seemed especially inclined toward brash and in-your-face responses that turned the threat back on the president. On signs carried by young marchers, a uterus and Fallopian tubes gave Trump the finger or transformed into the liberty-defending Gadsden flag rattlesnake,[5] which declares, "Don't tread on me!" In another transformation, the Gadsden snake coiled around an umbrella handle with the caption "Don't pee on me," in parody of Trump's rumored request for "golden showers." The vagina dentata, traditional symbol of women's violent, castrating power (Otero 2008), crunches Trump in his guise

Vagina dentata crunching Cheeto Trump, Washington, DC. Photo by Maxine Vande Vaarst.

"A woman's place is in the Resistance."
Raleigh, North Carolina. Photo by
Patricia Sawin.

as a Cheeto. Many marchers decried Trump's self-declared entitlement to grab women's genitals, insisting, "This pussy grabs back," "Don't even think about it," or "Regarding my pussy: No grabbing!" One young woman in Raleigh costumed herself as a tiger and displayed a painting of an attacking tiger, suggesting how dangerous such "grabbing" could be. Other signs pushed back against Trump's attempts to normalize unacceptable sexist behavior: "Boys will be ~~boys~~ good human beings."

Younger marchers drew especially on empowering popular culture references. Many signs depicted the Star Wars characters Ren and Princess Leia, asserting, "A woman's place is in the Resistance," "The Fempire Strikes Back," and "We'll never give in to the Dark Side." A number of photos widely circulated on social media showed children and young people carrying signs with a slogan popular among feminist Harry Potter fans, "Without Hermione, Harry would've died in Book 1." Representations of Wonder Woman and other female comic book superheroes exemplified women's power.

While these signs were amusing at one level, they also did serious philosophical work, insisting that while inspiration and rallying points may differ among generations, they can be powerful wherever they exist. The young were already criticizing the president's undisciplined, provocative, and frankly unpresidential social media use, with signs accessorized with the blue Twitter bird logo and demanding "Tweet us with respect," "Off with his thumb," or "OMFG Stop Tweeting!" Signs arguing that enough

"Fempire strikes back." Denver. Photo by Karen Deal Robinson.

"snowflakes" would create an avalanche or that "Winter is coming" most directly confronted conservatives who have mocked young people as weak for insisting upon trigger warnings and sensitivity to trauma. Yet they also, whether intentionally or not, emphasized to older marchers the value of young people's participation in the movement.

Some marchers in the maiden cohort—those well versed in intersectional feminism from their university or graduate studies—were also particularly aware of the political limitations of

"We'll never give in to the dark side."

Denver. Photo by Karen Deal Robinson.

"OMFG stop Tweeting," Washington, DC. Photo by Maxine Vande Vaarst.

Women superheroes, Denver. Photo by Karen Deal Robinson.

an action initially dreamed up by a group of white, middle-class women. A friend in Chicago reflected that she "felt very aware of my own privilege, and that though I am angry, I'm not personally likely to be threatened by this administration because of my resources, skin color, and abilities, etc., . . . [while] . . . Trump's election signified a real de-valuing of anyone who is not white." An anthropologist who works in the Black Caribbean noted, "I never got the smug satisfaction of the pink pussy hats (which smacked of white feminism, and not all vaginas are pink, and I don't think I want to self-identify as a vagina anyway) so that part was alienating to me." A graduate student who marched in DC explained, "I felt conflicted about the march's commodification of feminism and its struggle to critique white feminism." She recalled that "brushing against speaker Rep. Maxine Waters was exciting, but I was disturbed by the time limit imposed on other speakers, particularly . . . on a trans woman of color."

Despite these sentiments, those in this cohort seemed the most exhilarated during the march. For example, graduate student Maxine Vande Vaarst recalled her experience in the DC march in a paper she wrote later that semester and shared with me:

> There were hundreds and hundreds of thousands of people, so many that at times we couldn't move. There was no exit. There was no cell signal. You carried only what you brought with you, and the rest of the world dissolved into the now. All that was left was

us, friendly faces and shining people in every direction. The police stood down. The right-wingers were politely shooed back into their caves. We stomped along the middle of Constitution Avenue, and we climbed up lampposts and we jumped on top of trucks. We filled in the bleachers that had sat mostly empty for the previous day's inaugural parade. Everything was ours, and everything was working. "Show me what democracy looks like," they demanded of us. "This is what democracy looks like," we shouted back. All of the misery and confusion that had eaten at our hearts for ten weeks since the election disappeared, or better, it transformed. It was a new energy, new passion, new anger, new optimism. And we believed in it.

Some younger marchers were also especially savvy about the practicalities of participation in a protest in ways that those who engage less frequently (if ever) were not. A graduate student with a background in sound design explained how she had strategically planned the whole day in DC for herself and her parents, including a very early start, in order to position them relative to some of the giant audio speakers on the Mall and give the best chance of hearing and understanding the speeches.

The cohort whom I identify as mothers (and fathers), and who, indeed, identified themselves as such with their signs or comments, emphasized that they participated in the march because of the effect upon their children (immediate or eventual). Jon Nichols, a father who marched in Oakland, California, with his wife and nine-year-old daughter explained that one of his motivations was "modeling decency for my kid" and reported, "My daughter wore a pussy hat and it got me close to tears seeing her chanting the same kinds of things I've been chanting at protests for 35 years." Celeste Gagnon, who brought her twelve-year-old daughter from New Jersey to the march in Washington, noted, "Most memorable was my daughter's exhilaration of seeing so many different kinds of people coming together. This was her first experience of a large-scale event and seeing the power of collective action." Maria Schumann marched with her ten-year-old son in Montpelier, Vermont: "The streets were alive and bustling with other people . . . [My] son . . . had his drum, and he found his way to a super cool drumming contingent. He has Down syndrome, so sometimes just walking with him can feel like a statement. He is so alive and beautiful and loves drumming and parades so much; I felt so proud to be walking with him." My own then-twelve-year-old daughter despises Trump primarily because his racist anti-immigration policies make her Latinx friends fear discrimination or even deportation. Still, she came along to the march with her father and me and a couple of our friends most unwillingly, grumbling, "Adults caused this mess; you fix it." I remain hopeful that she will eventually understand the point of our being part of the protest—and maybe even appreciate my insistence.

Those in the parent cohort tended toward signs that were clever but earnest rather than rudely confrontational, sometimes but not always specifically referencing their parental role. A dad in Raleigh carried a sign asserting that it is not just girls' futures we are fighting for: "My daughter deserves better than this. So do my sons. I'm not giving up." Schumann, a sheep farmer from Vermont, glued wool onto burlap for a sheep-themed sign: "We are not sheep. We wool fight ewe and your billionaire henchmen and your nefarious quest to steal from the poor and destroy the planet." Gagnon brainstormed with her daughter for their poster: "We are the wall against hate." Nichols created a small, elegant sign stating simply, "Emoluments clause."

For parents, it was important not only to oppose Trump's destructive policies and attitudes that they feared would compromise their children's futures but also to prepare their children to carry on the fight for themselves. And it was not only those who are already parents or grandparents who had this in mind. Sleight-Price explained her participation in the Women's Marches of 2017 and 2018 and other subsequent protests: "I also march not for the present but also for the future; I'm not a parent yet, but hopefully someday I will be, and I want my posterity to know that their mother/grandmother/aunt/great-aunt, etc., stood with immigrants, and people of all colors, religions and genders."

Elder marchers often also identified as parents or grandparents and shared parental concerns, but we crones—enacting our role as wise and even ruthless truth tellers—played several distinctive roles crucial to the mood and message of the march. Crones extended parental devotion beyond one's particular family. I, for example (not currently a grandmother, but of an appropriate age), created a sign with a *Goodnight Moon* parody I'd found on Facebook: "Goodnight Obama, Goodnight Moon, Goodnight legally unrestricted womb, Goodnight science, Goodnight facts, Goodnight corporate income tax, Goodnight stars, Goodnight air, Goodnight equal rights everywhere," to which I had added, "We'll write a BETTER story for ALL our children." Elder marchers could display their wisdom with age's privilege of bluntness. A Los Angeles marcher went for the direct and simple, carrying a sign saying, "NOT MY PRESIDENT," a photo of him with a red circle and a diagonal line through the photo. Others positioned themselves as the most serious arbiters of decent behavior. A white-haired woman in Raleigh had created a sign declaring, "Greatness demands knowledge, compassion, integrity." Many in the crone cohort chose to claim the moral and intellectual high ground by suggesting their intelligence and sophistication in contrast to

Leedom Lefferts holding the sign with which Patricia Sawin marched, "Goodnight, Obama, Goodnight moon . . ." Raleigh, North Carolina. Photo by Patricia Sawin.

that of the newly inaugurated national leader and by pointedly eschewing profanity (with the occasional crucial exception). A Raleigh marcher parodied Trump's plan to expand the wall along the US-Mexico border and his senseless boast that he would "get Mexico to pay for it" with a sign reading, "Build a wall around Trump. We'll pay for it." Others calmly looked above the fray by advocating for specific causes dear to them that might not have been in the front of most people's minds. Barry Bergey, former director of the Folk and Traditional Arts section of the National Endowment for the Arts, marched in Washington, DC, with a punning sign insisting, "Hands Off the pARTS." While lending a certain dignity and composure to the protest, crones with gray or white hair sticking out from under many a pussy hat simultaneously evoked Rabelais's carnivalesque—turning the world (and especially the world we feared Trump would create) upside down by exemplifying energy out of decrepitude if not quite life out of death (Bakhtin 1968). By our very presence in the streets, at the Women's March, and under the undeniably sexual symbol of the pussy hat, crones utterly rejected the sexist insistence that women must appear perpetually young, attractive, and submissive. Older marchers who may have worried that they were not up to the physical rigors of the march celebrated discovering that they were. A woman in her seventies reported:

> The Los Angeles March was huge, and the numbers of people funneling down the streets from every direction and pouring in to join the march was thrilling, heartening, and validating. There were so many people that we could not hear the speakers and it was hard for the march to get going, but this did not matter. We were all there in cohesiveness. It was so energizing that I was not ever tired, and could have continued for hours more.

Even those of us who were tired or cold or uncertain what exactly we were supposed to be doing demonstrated by perseverance that we were not going anywhere (in multiple senses).

Crones served crucial roles as repositories of wisdom and historical comparison and reminders of the long history of protest. Jean Renfro Anspaugh explained:

> I was in the March on Washington for the Moratorium to end the War in Vietnam back in October 1969. I have been marching on Washington since I was a teenager. I marched this time for my granddaughter—Chloe—so she could have choices and opportunities and own her own body and control her destiny—not a bunch of men in the White House and Congress.

And when her resolve about participating in the march wavered, Anspaugh's husband reenergized her by reminding her of her lengthy dedication to protest. "He said, 'What, are you going to stop now?'" to which she responded, "'No, I am not stopping.'" Karen Robinson and her adult daughter held hands to keep from getting separated at the Denver march and sang the "Sister Suffragettes" song from *Mary Poppins*—whimsical and special to their family, yet a potent reminder that the Women's March was just one in a long series of women's struggles for rights and respect. Another Los Angeles marcher in her seventies reported: "Those of us (older) folks who had marched years ago protesting the Vietnam War recognized each other, and connected around our willingness to protest again." Lefferts started marching with my group of friends, then disappeared into the Raleigh crowd to join up with fellow Vietnam era members of Veterans for Peace.

Barry Bergey holding his "Hands off the pARTS" sign, Washington, DC. Photo by Jean Bergey.

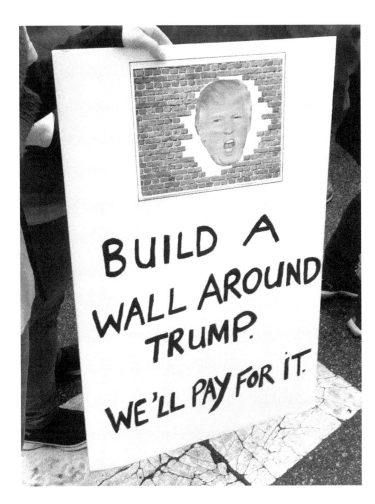

"Build a wall around Trump. We'll pay for it." Raleigh, North Carolina. Photo by Leedom Lefferts.

Some older marchers, perhaps not quite crones, played an inverse role, emphasizing that they were not building on long experience as protestors. The woman in Denver carrying a sign reading "60 years old!!! First protest!!! Many more to come!!!" portrayed herself as an elder who—for reasons unspecified—finally recognized a need or an opportunity for her to participate in protest. The most poignant story I heard about the march came from a student who marched with her parents, aunt, and uncle, all of whom had been involved in civil rights and anti–Vietnam War protests. Despite crowds so large that the student and her family were almost not allowed into the DC Metro station to try to get to the Mall, her mother continued to worry that (in contrast to struggles past) no one would really show up for the Women's March. When the train pulled in, every car already crammed with women in pink pussy hats, she burst into tears of relief.

My favorite elders' signs displayed knowledge born of historical perspective—how many rights women have gained in the past fifty years, what is was like to live (and sometimes die) without those rights and legal protections, how hard the struggle has been, and how precarious many of those now-established rights already were in the face of the right-wing backlash. Some crones simply expressed determination: "I won't go quietly back to the 1950s"; others, disgust: "I can't believe I *still* have to protest this shit!" It is worth noting that the "I can't believe . . ." slogan was not original to the Women's March. It has been used for a number of years especially in protests for

reproductive rights and equal pay, sometimes by protestors dressed in costumes intended to evoke nineteenth-century women's rights crusaders or suffragettes. It gained a particular appropriateness in the January 2017 context, however, highlighting not just delay in achieving women's equality but the specific threats Trump had made to rescind hard-won women's and LGBTQ rights. Interestingly—as I discovered when I asked friends and colleagues to send me a photograph of someone carrying the "I can't believe" sign to use for this article—some of those representing themselves as

"60 years old. First protest. Many more to come." Denver. Photo by Karen Deal Robinson.

"I will _not_ go quietly back to the 1950s." Raleigh, North Carolina. Photo by Leedom Lefferts.

frustrated about "still protest[ing] this shit" were quite young. I am not sure whether to be heartened that the rising generation does not want to wait any longer for women's equality or concerned that they will need to develop patience for what, if history and the current ascendance of a hateful Right are guides, may still be a long fight.

While I find the distinctions among age cohorts significant, it is important to remember that those participating in the march experienced these mostly as variety, not division. The march was so symbolically, morally, and emotionally rich precisely because people marched or stood or rode buses or carpooled along with those older and younger. Mary Bell in Denver reported that she marched with four generations of her family, from her eighty-year-old self down to a three-year-old great-granddaughter. One of my Los Angeles respondents in her seventies said her most significant memory was of "the kindness and consideration and camaraderie of fellow marchers of all ages, genders, gender orientations, religions, ethnic origins, skin colors." Despite moments of uncertainty or discomfort, the lasting impression of the day for most participants was of *communitas*, as Edith Turner explains it, that sense of joy and connection "felt by a group of people when their life together takes on full meaning," when people are ready "to rid themselves of their concern for status and dependence on structures and see their fellows as they are" (2012:1–2; see also Victor Turner 1974:76–77).

Communitas does not last beyond the intense moment of togetherness (1974:78), but the memory can be inspiring. The sense of having been at one with so many thousands of other different people is likely part of what has induced some march participants to get more involved in organizations that support the causes in which they believe or to work for political candidates. While much march signage admonished the new administration, it became clear to participants that we were one another's primary audience at the time and going forward. As Sleight-Price explained,

"I can't believe I still have to protest this shit." Atlanta. Photo by Lisa Cremin.

I march because my neighbors need to know which side I'm on. I don't think #45 cares one bit about whether or not I am out freezing in the streets every January to show my distaste for him and his hateful rhetoric/policies, but maybe, just maybe my participation can be part of the broader discussions that need to be taking place at the constituency level.

Generational differences could be a barrier to *communitas* at times. Graduate student Elaine Yau, who marched in San Francisco, recalled that when Joan Baez sang "in English and Spanish," older marchers engaged eagerly with a familiar song that had inspired many of them through earlier protests, while the marchers of younger generations stood uncomfortably, not knowing how to respond. Conversely, Yau and her friends became energized and started moving once the march played a Beyoncé song and reacted with enthusiasm and joy to a group of Afro-Cuban drummers. Brief moments of unease did not rupture an overall feeling of cooperation, however. It further intrigues me that none of my older respondents mentioned being made uncomfortable by unfamiliar newer music. Perhaps experience tells you to expect that in a multigenerational gathering not everything will be familiar to your cohort.

Like traditional calendrical revelers—mummers (Glassie 1975), Belsnickles (Bauman 1972), and participants in country Mardi Gras (Sawin 2001)—marchers simultaneously turned the status quo (at least that upon which the new administration insisted) upside down and

Young protester carrying "I cannot believe I still have to protest this shit" sign, Palais de Chaillot, Paris. Photo by Theresa Vaughan.

established the boundaries of our territory, insisting that we are here—in symbolic political spaces like the nation's capital and in the practical downtowns of hundreds of cities—to stay. Like the costumed protestors of New York's anti-rent wars (Saltzman 1994), we defined and demanded moral behavior via sometimes outrageous demonstration. One might even trace a similarity to Gerald Vizenor's concept of American Indian "survivance," the determination to operate on the basis of one's own values, history, and beliefs, even in situations where their validity is unrecognized or denied (2008). Like a native elder's making a land claim on the basis of sacred stories (whether or not the judge appointed by the colonizer government will treat these as evidence),[6] the women and allies who marched insisted that our humane and feminist values are the standard on which the universe operates, regardless of the heedless and profane practices of the current administration. The mood of the marchers and our sense of hope and potential were well summarized by signs declaring, "The power of the people is greater than the people in power."

Still, the noticeable presence of members of different generations was crucial to the experience and message of the march. Together we rang the changes on Judith Butler's sense of gender identity as a recursive performance (1990), insisting that each of us in our uniqueness and all of us collectively created valid versions of and models for what it means to be a woman, a person to be valued, listened to, and respected at every stage of life. Babies and children exemplified the innocence and vulnerability for which the new administration seemed to have no regard and insisted that we were fighting not merely for ourselves but for future generations. Young people exhibited raw determination and the willingness both to mock the new president's unacceptable (yet somehow, by his own party, accepted) behavior and to fight back in his own profane tone. Parents exemplified the power of those called to protect those they love. Older people had the standing to criticize the (elderly) president's immaturity and lack of discipline, reminded those younger that crucial social change requires patience and persistence, and demanded that we not go backward to reimpose discriminatory and destructive social policies that so many had fought so long to correct.

Establishing respect and common cause among the generations was also a corrective to any lingering distrust among women who have held differing opinions about how to claim women's rights. Older feminists, myself included, have been puzzled by or even dismissive of millennial women who (especially a decade or so ago) told us they believed in men and women's social and economic equality yet insisted that there was no longer a need to call themselves feminists. Presumably some of these swelled the ranks of the parental and older maiden cohorts, their minds having been changed by the new president's explicit misogyny. During the presidential campaign just disappointingly concluded, conversely, some younger and more radical feminists' appreciation of intersectional identities and critique of capitalism had led them to support Bernie Sanders over Hillary Clinton in the primaries and to criticize Clinton's and the Democratic Party's ties to the wealthy. While most agreed that Madeleine Albright's and Gloria Steinem's insistence that all women were morally bound to support the female candidate had been narrow and counterproductive, the dispute still rankled (Cummins 2016). Younger feminists had then leveled their intersectional critique at the march itself, questioning whether a women's March would depend upon an outmoded, white-centric and heteronormative model of universal womanhood. Their insistence had pushed the group of white women who had dreamed up the idea for the march to broaden the leadership across lines of race, ethnicity, religion, immigration status, sexuality, and trans-identity. Those efforts—even if they did not solve all shortcomings or satisfy all critics—and the energetic participation of people across the age spectrum represented an important effort at bridge building. Arguably, the march was a feminist fourth-wave phenomenon (see Chamberlain 2017:2). It was organized via social media. It drew in not only long-standing feminists (who have focused on women's legal and reproductive rights) but also younger women (whose opposition to rape culture made them especially horrified by the new president's impunity). And it was characterized both by the insistence upon an intersectional perspective that made the march more inclusive and by the humor that buoyed our collective energies. In marching together, reading and appreciating one another's signs, and taking and sharing photos with friends in other marches in other cities, women and allies of a range of ages had the opportunity to "reject the linear and generational aspects of the [feminist] narrative, which encourage a mother–daughter divisiveness" (Chamberlain 2017:45). In the *communitas* of the march, we became a single wave, renouncing divisive countercurrents, carrying forward a panoply of progressive causes, and offering our mutual support for one another's crucial ongoing efforts.

Notes

1. The Twenty-sixth Amendment to the Constitution, changing the national voting age from twenty-one to eighteen, was passed in 1971. The argument "Old enough to fight, old enough to vote" was raised during the Second World War but was finally successful during the Vietnam conflict (History.com).

2. I have chosen for this brief essay to focus on the question of generational distinctiveness but recognize the importance of a wider topic that I have not explored: the extent to which the Women's March, initially dreamed up by a group of white friends, managed to include and represent women across lines of race, class, sexuality, and cis- or trans-status.

3. Political scientists Jeremy Pressman of the University of Connecticut and Erica Chenoweth, at the time of the March at the University of Denver, now of the Harvard Kennedy School, created a spreadsheet on which they recorded locations of marches and crowd counts from local and press reports, then averaged high and low estimates. This was an evolving online source that was exciting to watch in the hours and days just after the Women's March as the scale of participation became evident. Their "best guess" is that 4,157,894 people marched in the United States (1.28% of the population of 324,753,103 on January 21, 2017, according to the US Census Population Clock) and another 357,748 marchers in other countries, for a total of 4,515,642.

4. I received verbal accounts from people who marched in Chicago; Denver; Eugene, Oregon; Los Angeles; Montpelier, Vermont; Oakland, California;

Park City, Utah; Raleigh; San Francisco; and Washington, DC. I thank all my respondents. Those who gave me permission to mention them by name are: Jean Renfro Anspaugh, Mary Bell, Susan Eleuterio, Celeste Gagnon, Rachel Rae Miller, Jon Nichols, Kathleen Nichols, Karen Deal Robinson, Maria Schumann, Camille Sleight-Price, Shannon Slepak-Cherney, Maxine Vande Vaarst, and Elaine Yau.

5. The Gadsden flag, with a green rattlesnake on a yellow ground and the motto "Don't Tread on Me," was created by Christopher Gadsden, a Charleston-born brigadier general in the Continental Army. It was the most enduring of several anti-British, prorevolution flags used in the colonies during the Revolutionary War. While the creators of the Women's March signs were likely thinking about the original uses of the image, since the 1970s the flag became popular in Libertarian circles and was then adopted by the Tea Party. Under the Obama administration it "picked up other connotations: strident anti-government sentiment, often directed with particular vehemence at the first African-American President" (Walker 2016). These feminist, anti-Trump usages thus might be considered also a reclamation of the symbol.

6. See Matson 2004 for discussion of a Canadian First Nations land claims case in which the judge allowed months of testimony that sought to establish a claim on the basis of tribal legends but then declared only written documents (all produced by European settlers) valid evidence. That verdict was overturned by the appeals court.

Works Cited

Bakhtin, Mikhail M. 1968. *Rabelais and His World.* Bloomington: Indiana University Press.

Bakhtin, Mikhail M. 1981. *The Dialogic Imagination.* Austin: University of Texas Press.

Bauman, Richard. 1972. Belsnickling in a Nova Scotia Island Community. *Western Folklore* 31(4):229–43.

Butler, Judith. 1990. *Gender Trouble: Feminism and the Subversion of Identity.* New York: Routledge.

Chamberlain, Prudence. 2017. *The Feminist Fourth Wave: Affective Temporality.* Palgrave Macmillan US.

Cummins, Denise. 2016. Why Millennial Women Don't Want to Call Themselves Feminists. *PBS News Hour*, February 12. https://www.pbs.org/newshour/economy/column-why-millennial-women-dont-want-to-call-themselves-feminists.

Glassie, Henry. 1983. *All Silver and No Brass: An Irish Christmas Mumming.* Philadelphia: University of Pennsylvania Press. Originally published 1975.

History.com. The 26th Amendment. https://www.history.com/topics/the-26th-amendment.

Matson, Elizabeth Ann. 2004. History Spoken Aloud: The Implications of the Supreme Court of Canada's Ruling on Oral History in *Delgamuukw v. The Queen*. Master's thesis, Folklore Program, University of North Carolina.

Otero, Solimar. 2008. Vagina Dentata. In *Encyclopedia of Women's Folklore and Folklife*, edited by Liz Locke, Theresa A. Vaughan, and Pauline Greenhill, 669–70. Santa Barbara, CA: ABC-CLIO.

Piven, Frances Fox. 2006. *Challenging Authority: How Ordinary People Change America*. Lanham, MD: Rowman and Littlefield.

Piven, Frances Fox. 2014. The Structuring of Protest. In *Who's Afraid of Frances Fox Piven? The Essential Writings of the Professor Glenn Beck Loves to Hate*, pp. 67–102. New York: New Press. Originally published 1977.

Pressman, Jeremy, and Chenoweth, Erica. 2017. Women's March Attendance Estimate Spreadsheet (closed January 26, 2017; accessed October 14, 2017). https://docs.google.com/spreadsheets/d/1xaoiLqYKz8x9Yc_rfhtmSOJQ2EG geUVjvV4A8LsIaxY/htmlview?sle=true#gid=0.

Saltzman, Rachelle H. 1994. Calico Indians and Pistol Pills: Traditional Drama, Historical Symbols, and Political Actions in Upstate New York. *New York Folklore* 3–4:1–17.

Sawin, Patricia. 2001. Transparent Masks: The Ideology and Practice of Disguise in Contemporary Cajun Mardi Gras. *Journal of American Folklore* 114(452):175–203.

Turner, Edith. 2012. *Communitas: The Anthropology of Collective Joy*. New York: Palgrave Macmillan.

Turner, Victor. 1974. Liminal to Liminoid in Play, Flow, and Ritual. *Rice University Studies* 60(3):53–92.

US Census Population Clock. https://www.census.gov/popclock/.

Vizenor, Gerald. 2008. *Survivance: Narratives of Native Presence*. Lincoln: University of Nebraska Press.

Walker, Rob. 2016. The Shifting Symbolism of the Gadsden Flag. *New Yorker*. October 2. https://www.newyorker.com/news/news-desk/the-shifting-symbolism-of-the-gadsden-flag.

Wanshel, Elyse. 2017. This #WokeBaby Made Her Own Adorable Sign for the Women's March. *Huffpost: Parenting*, January 23. https://www.huffington post.com/entry/toddler-protest-sign-womens-march-washington-charlotte _us_58861fcce4b096b4a2330682.

Women's March Organizers and Condé Nast. 2018. *Together We Rise: The Women's March: Behind the Scenes at the Protest Heard around the World*. New York: Dey Street.

CONTRIBUTORS

SUSAN ELEUTERIO is a professional folklorist, educator, and consultant to nonprofits and serves as an adjunct faculty member of Goucher College's Masters in Cultural Sustainability program. She has a master's in American Folk Culture from the Cooperstown Graduate Program (SUNY/Oneonta) and a BA in English/Education (University of Delaware). Eleuterio is the Co-Chair of the Chicago-based Crossroads Fund Board of Directors, serves as a board member for Illinois Humanities, and was a workshop leader and board member for the Neighborhood Writing Alliance in Chicago for over ten years. Eleuterio is the author of *Irish American Material Culture: A Directory of Collections, Sites and Festivals in the United States and Canada*, as well as numerous peer-reviewed essays and a collaboratively written chapter in *Comfort Food, Meanings and Memories* (University Press of Mississippi, 2017). Eleuterio has conducted fieldwork and developed public programs including exhibits, performances, folk arts education workshops and residencies in schools, along with professional development programs for teachers, students, adults, and artists for schools, museums, arts education agencies and arts organizations across the United States.

ANDREA GLASS is an instructor in the Women and Gender Studies Department at the University of Delaware. Her doctorate in American Studies from Pennsylvania State University focuses on urban culture and folklore, gender and sexuality, and place-based identity. Glass holds master's degrees from the University of Delaware and Pennsylvania State University as well as a bachelor's from the latter. She has presented her research widely at a variety of national conferences, including the annual meetings of the American Folklore Society (AFS), the American Academy of Religion (AAR), and the Popular Culture Association/American Culture Association (PCA/ACA). In 2013 she was the recipient of the Bill Ellis Award from the New Directions in Folklore section of AFS. Glass has published "Scenes through the Rear-View Mirror: 1970s New York and the Cultural and Spatial Influence of Martin Scorsese's *Taxi Driver*" in the *Journal of Popular Film and Television*, and "'I Want to Be a Witness': Blogging for Urban Authenticity and Cultural Authority in the East Village," in *New Directions in Folklore*. She is currently working on a book-length project entitled *Narratives of Loss: Documenting Place-Based Identity, Vanishing Landscapes, and the War on Gentrification in Urban America*.

RACHELLE H. (RIKI) SALTZMAN served as Executive Director of the Oregon Folklife Network, the state's Folk and Traditional Arts Program from 2012–20; she is now a consulting folklorist for OFN and the High Desert Museum. Her interests range from food and place to ethnic identity and cultural heritage. As a lecturer in Folklore and Public Culture at the University of Oregon, she teaches classes in public folklore, and food and folklore. Since 1983 she has worked as a public folklorist in seven states and with the Smithsonian Institution; she has produced a radio series, exhibits, websites, festivals, and conferences. Prior to coming to Oregon, she was the Folklife Coordinator for the Iowa Arts Council for nearly two decades. Saltzman, who obtained her PhD in Anthropology (Folklore) from the University of Texas at Austin, has written numerous public folklore publications as well as peer-reviewed articles in professional journals and books. She is the author of *A Lark for the Sake of Their Country: The 1926 General Strike Volunteers in Folklore and Memory* (2012, Manchester University Press).

JACK SANTINO is a professor of folklore and popular culture at Bowling Green State University. He was the Alexis de Tocqueville Distinguished Professor at the University of Paris–Sorbonne, 2010–2011. He was a Fulbright scholar to Northern Ireland and has conducted research in Spain and France. His documentary film on Pullman porters, *Miles of Smiles, Years of Struggle*, received four Emmy awards. He has been President of the American Folklore Society and Editor of the *Journal of American Folklore*. His research focusses on rituals and celebrations, with a particular interest in carnival and political and public ritual. He is the author of numerous books and articles, including *Public Performances: Studies in the Carnivalesque and the Ritualesque* (USU Press, 2017); *Spontaneous Shrines and the Public Memorialization of Death* (Palgrave Macmillan, 2006); and *Signs of War and Peace: Social Conflict and the Uses of Symbols in Public in Northern Ireland* (Palgrave Macmillan, 2002).

PATRICIA SAWIN is an associate professor, Department of American Studies, University of North Carolina, Chapel Hill, and Coordinator of the Folklore master's degree program. She is the author of "'Every Kid Is Where They're Supposed to Be, and It's a Miracle': Family Formation Stories among Adoptive Families" (*Journal of American Folklore*, 2017)w, "Performance at the Nexus of Gender, Power, and Desire" (Journal of American Folklore 2002), "Transparent Masks: The Ideology and Practice of Masking in Cajun Country Mardi Gras" (*Journal of American Folklore*, 2001), and numerous articles and book chapters on performance, personal narrative, festival, and the culture of adoption. She has also published *Listening for a Life: A Dialogic Ethnography of Bessie Eldreth through Her Songs and Stories* (Utah State University Press, 2004).

ADAM ZOLKOVER is an instructional designer for the Department of Medical Ethics and Health Policy at the University of Pennsylvania's Perelman School of Medicine. He holds a master's in Folklore from Indiana University, Bloomington. He has taught courses on American folklore, folklore and popular culture, and folk narrative, and written about those topics, as well as the history of folkloristics. At present, his research focuses on students' experience of community in online courses and on best practices for fostering collaboration online.

INDEX

Page numbers in *italics* indicate an illustration.